"Have you ever considered the way experience that goes unregistered or unsymbolized – the unformulated, the somatic, the unthought known, the 'something more' – might be both shaped by, and contribute to shaping, clinical process? Have you thought about psychoanalysis as the creation, via this kind of work, of 'communion' with the other, and eventually a sense of community? These are the crucial themes explored by Steven Knoblauch in this book. Today, with increasing awareness that psychoanalysis must attend as much to our embeddedness in cultures as it does to traditional individual development, this message is as timely as it is fascinating."

Donnel B. Stern, PhD, William Alanson White Institute and NYU Postdoctoral Program in Psychoanalysis and Psychotherapy

"Since the publication of his first book, Steven Knoblauch has expanded our ideas about the musicalities of psychoanalytic engagement. In *Bodies and Social Rhythms*, he establishes himself as not only a creative theorist, but as a thorough historian of psychoanalytic thought. He writes personally, guiding us through his own development as a clinician and theorist whose feet are firmly planted in ideals of both psychoanalytic and community-based action and communion. This book offers a wonderfully rich history of psychoanalytic notions of attachment and symbolization, but they are held in a constant tension with the social. He ends by turning to Fanon in a chapter that is a must-read for anyone attempting to come to grips with the ways the social and the unconscious co-mingle to support or disrupt communion and recognition."

Katie Gentile, PhD, Professor of Gender Studies, Chair, Department of Interdisciplinary Studies, John Jay College of Criminal Justice, CUNY

"The focus of this book is the amazing expansion in the psychoanalytic horizon when attending to micro-moments of the embodied emotional flux and rhythms that manifest the unconscious non-symbolic experience. Clinical dense descriptions of these micro-moments demonstrate how embodied gestures are also determined by the cultural and social context that extends beyond analyst and patient. Preserving

D0217094

its value, the author questions the restrictions of the structural cognitive frame that has predominated in psychoanalysis. A frame that has defended from the vulnerability inherent in surrendering to the porousness of shared bodies. A must-read to acknowledge the curative power that lies dormant beyond interpretation."

Juan Francisco Jordan-Moore, MD, Psychiatrist, Psychoanalyst, President IARPP-Chile, Attached Associate Professor, Psychology School of the Catholic University of Chile, Member IARPP Board

Bodies and Social Rhythms

This exciting new book traces the development of an unfolding challenge for psychoanalytic attention, which augments contemporary theoretical lenses focusing on structures of meaning, with an accompanying registration different than and interacting with structural experience. This accompanying registration of experience is given the term "fluidity" in order to characterize it as too fast-moving and unformulated to be symbolized with linguistic categorization.

Expanding attention from speech meaning to include embodied registrations of rhythm involving tonality, pauses and accents can catalyze additional and often emotionally more significant communications central to the state of the transactional field in any psychoanalytic moment. This perspective is contextualized within recognition of how cultural practices and beliefs are carried along both structural and fluid registrations of experience and can shape emotional turbulence for both interactants in a clinical encounter. Experiences of gender, culture, class and race emerging as sources of conflict and mis-recognition are engaged and illustrated throughout the text.

This book, part of the popular "Psychoanalysis in a New Key" book series, will appeal to teaching and practicing psychoanalysts, but also an increasing volume of therapists attending to embodied experience in their practice and drawn to the practical clinical illustrations.

Steven H. Knoblauch, PhD, is a Clinical Adjunct Associate Professor at the Postdoctoral Program in Psychotherapy and Psychoanalysis, New York University. He is author of *The Musical Edge of Therapeutic Dialogue* (2000) and a co-author of *Forms of Intersubjectivity in Infant Research and Adult Treatment* (2005).

PSYCHOANALYSIS IN A NEW KEY BOOK SERIES

When music is played in a new key, the melody does not change, but the notes that make up the composition do: change in the context of continuity, continuity that perseveres through change. Psychoanalysis in a New Key publishes books that share the aims psychoanalysts have always had, but that approach them differently. The books in the series are not expected to advance any particular theoretical agenda, although to this date most have been written by analysts from the Interpersonal and Relational orientations.

The most important contribution of a psychoanalytic book is the communication of something that nudges the reader's grasp of clinical theory and practice in an unexpected direction. Psychoanalysis in a New Key creates a deliberate focus on innovative and unsettling clinical thinking. Because that kind of thinking is encouraged by exploration of the sometimes surprising contributions to psychoanalysis of ideas and findings from other fields, Psychoanalysis in a New Key particularly encourages interdisciplinary studies. Books in the series have married psychoanalysis with dissociation, trauma theory, sociology, and criminology. The series is open to the consideration of studies examining the relationship between psychoanalysis and any other field – for instance, biology, literary, and art criticism, philosophy, systems theory, anthropology, and political theory.

But innovation also takes place within the boundaries of psychoanalysis, and Psychoanalysis in a New Key therefore also presents work that reformulates thought and practice without leaving the precincts of the field. Books in the series focus, for example, on the significance of personal values in psychoanalytic practice, on the complex interrelationship between the analyst's clinical work and personal life, on the consequences for the clinical situation when patient and analyst are from different cultures, and on the need for psychoanalysts to accept the degree to which they knowingly satisfy their own wishes during treatment hours, often to the patient's detriment A full list of all titles in this series is available at: www.routledge.com/series/LEAPNKBS

Bodies and Social Rhythms

Navigating Unconscious Vulnerability and Emotional Fluidity

Steven H. Knoblauch

 Routledge
Taylor & Francis Group

LONDON AND NEW YORK

First published 2021
by Routledge
2 Park Square, Milton Park, Abingdon, Oxon OX14 4RN

and by Routledge
52 Vanderbilt Avenue, New York, NY 10017

Routledge is an imprint of the Taylor & Francis Group, an informa business

© 2021 Steven H. Knoblauch

The right of Steven H. Knoblauch to be identified as author of this
work has been asserted by him in accordance with sections 77 and 78
of the Copyright, Designs and Patents Act 1988.

All rights reserved. No part of this book may be reprinted or
reproduced or utilised in any form or by any electronic, mechanical,
or other means, now known or hereafter invented, including
photocopying and recording, or in any information storage or retrieval
system, without permission in writing from the publishers.

Trademark notice: Product or corporate names may be trademarks or
registered trademarks, and are used only for identification and
explanation without intent to infringe.

British Library Cataloguing-in-Publication Data
A catalogue record for this book is available from the British Library

Library of Congress Cataloging-in-Publication Data
A catalog record has been requested for this book

ISBN: 978-0-367-46686-2 (hbk)
ISBN: 978-0-367-46685-5 (pbk)
ISBN: 978-1-003-03035-5 (ebk)

Typeset in Times
by Swales & Willis, Exeter, Devon, UK

For Lew Aron and my mother, Ruth Knoblauch.

Each of these wonderful human beings, who left us as this book unfolded, brought a love of humanity and relentless dedication to an appreciation of what others can teach.

Contents

Preface

While you and I are unavoidably embodied subjects and socially contextualized, we generally navigate these registrations of experience unconsciously. What is the relationship between these unconscious experiences and how we identify and relate? How do the body and the social impact our emotional vulnerability? What are the processes by which emotional vulnerability impacts identity formation and social affiliation(s)? How are these processes shaped by experiences of intersectionality as constructed or dissociated, abjected or valorized?

Registers of the body and the social shape the direction toward which I am stretching clinical attention with this text. At the same time, and despite my intention here, I acknowledge that the discursive culture in which I am constructing these chapters constrains my writing/thinking, often in terms of the binaries of thought/feeling, verbal/nonverbal, symbolized/embodied, and individual/collective. Throughout this text I struggle with these limitations. I address how these limitations constrict opportunities for vitalizing movement within and between myself and patients and how efforts to transcend these limitations, while always partial, open up into an expanded ecology for experience: both imaginative and interactive. In the last chapters of this text, I struggle with how the discourse of our craft is shaped and constricted by unconscious biases carried within the socially consensual terms and images we use to re-present psychoanalytic perspectives and strategies.

I am reaching here to move beyond the horizons of a lens concerned with categorical meanings alone, the interpretations in which psychoanalytic practitioners and patients trade. Rather, while still fairly grounded in the consulting room, this expansion in horizons for the imagination in tension with social experience, offers "something more." This "something more" is different than the term used by the Boston Change Process Study Group (2008). Their use of "something more" connotes a registration occurring on a micro-level of interaction. They focus on the micro-moment gestures, tones, and rhythms of infant/caregiver interaction as a model for framing patient/clinician interaction. I build on this micro-focus, distinguishing movement from structure. I am expanding the micro as a space/direction from which categories might emerge, to leave open the opportunity for "something more" in the fluidity of tensions that constitute the dense and swirling turbulence of unformulated emotions. These emotions in motion seem too complex and opaque for, but also so valuable in their resistance to the limitations of, categorization. How we might navigate these registrations which resist category/formulation, but which might be central to clinical opportunities, is the focus of this text.

But there is even something more to the "something more." Attention to micro-moment registrations of interactive experience brings into focus the ways that what is unformulated (Stern, 1997) is, nevertheless, present with significant affective impact. Additionally, psychoanalysts are now increasingly turning attention to the impact of the social on processes of internal representation as well as affective registrations of guilt, shame, powerlessness and various forms of socially constructed and contextualized abjection in addition to self-esteem and agency (See Fromm, 1941, 1947, 1955, 1962 for earlier considerations of these influences, as well as Guralnik, 2011, 2014a, 2014b, 2016; Layton, 2006; Philipson, 2017 and Rozmarin, 2017, for examples of contemporary discussions). These effects often have to do with hierarchical arrangements of power based on wealth and/or privileges emerging from racial, ethnic, class, and/or religious difference. And so "something more" is constituted not just by an expansion in micro-attention.

Now, in this time of light-speed communication and increasing ease of embodied travel across long distances in shorter and shorter times, there is much learning and sharing across what previously served as cultural barriers. But there is also an increase in fear, confusion, misunderstanding, and disagreement across different languages, beliefs, and practices, customary and marginalized. This is the realm of the "macro" which contextualizes and continuously interacts with the subjective experiences of patients and clinicians. In particular the socially driven effects of interpellation and dissociation become critical to both affective and cognitive experience as these effects abject or valorize, privilege or erase subjectivity.

D. N. Stern writes, "Communion means to share in another's experience with no attempt to change what that person is doing or believing" (Stern, 1985, p. 148). There is an emotional experience in communion that Emanuel Ghent (1990/1999) has described with the term "surrender." Surrender is distinguished from passive submission and seems to be an active availability and receptivity to the experiences of others (Knoblauch, 2005). Surrender makes possible communion. Communion is then the building block of community, the social dimension of experience. Community is then a continuously vitalizing, ongoing process and not a single thing, preplanned, prescribed (Nancy, 1986, 2000). Degree of communion shapes our beliefs and practices, our internal images and the polyrhythmicity and polyphony of the fluid cross modal registrations of our social rituals as expressed and experienced. Embodied experience takes place within an experience of community: a term which psychoanalysis is just beginning to explore (see Gonzalez, 2019a, Rozmarin, 2019). In this text I illustrate and explore the clinical relevance of opportunities for novelty and vitality as well as trauma emergent from the tensions, unconscious as well as conscious, between the embodied and the social as patients and practitioners struggle for communion.

Acknowledgments

This project is a product of community. While I serve as scribe, so many others have contributed to the ideas that I formulate in these next pages. First, I want to acknowledge the sufferings and achievements of my mother, Ruth and father, Leo, born of immigrants or first-generation Jewish folk. Located in Pennsylvania Deutsch country, they strove to achieve a higher education for themselves, positions of service to their communities as well as family, and opportunities for creation and service for myself, my brother, Ken and sister, Patti. Each of us chose the field of psychology, yet pursued it in different ways. I am grateful for the richness of our similarities and differences.

Second, I want to acknowledge my wife, Ingrid, a child psychologist, whose immigrant experience has continuously influenced my work; and my daughter, Giana, a uniquely attuned special-needs educator, each of whom have dedicated their talents to working with populations often misunderstood and underserved, yet so often having unique gifts to contribute to the families and communities in which they find themselves.

Third, I want to acknowledge the legions of friends, colleagues, and patients with whom I have shared so many adventures of suffering and triumph, always in the service of learning and growth. Unfortunately I could never adequately acknowledge the significance of your contributions to this project. We have worked and played, laughed and cried, together as folks discovering and pursuing our desires to live as simply fully human as possible. In particular, I offer thanks to those who contributed to the ideas in these chapters through conversation, reading and editing. Those whose influence most powerfully shaped my thinking, and whom I can publicly acknowledge herein, include Neil Altman, Fran Anderson, Lew Aron, Galit Atlas, Beatrice Beebe, Jessica Benjamin Kim Bernstein, Stephen Botticelli, Celia Brickman, Komal Choksi, Stephen Cooper, William Cornell, Jody Davies, Muriel Dimen, Katie Gentile, Adrienne Harris, Anton Hart, Stephen Hartman, Irwin Hoffman, Hazel Ipp, Annie Lee Jones, Lynne Layton, Steven Kuchuck, Stephen Mitchell, Gianni Nebbiosi and Susi Federici-Nebbiosi, Stephen Seligman, Sue Shapiro, Michelle Stephens, Daniel Stern, Donnel Stern, Melanie Suchet, Sally Swartz, John Edgar Wideman and Cleonie White.

Finally, I want to acknowledge the careful guidance and support from my editor Donnel Stern and the staff at Taylor & Francis, particularly the collaboration of Kate Hawes, Alec Selwyn, Simon Barraclough and Sonnie Wills. Their expertise and sensitivity to this work is invaluable to all of us in this field.

Steven H. Knoblauch PhD
September 13, 2019

Introduction

Formative influences

Socio-cultural influences

I came from a different world than Sigmund Freud, so it is no surprise that I feel and imagine my world quite differently than he did. George Atwood and Robert Stolorow (1993) addressed the significance of the way that a subject's unique personal and social history can unconsciously shape their professional pursuits and ways of organizing experience as their life unfolds. They gave this process the term *organizing principles* and examined the impact of such principles in the lives and works of Freud, Jung, Rank and Reich. I recognize, in my perspective, the limitations of the use of categories like the term organizing principles for phenomena that are, in fact, changing and fluid over time. So, though such phenomena may also exhibit structure and repetition, the chapters of this text reflect the importance I give to the struggle to hold both ways of experiencing in conscious tension. I believe such a vision can help to overcome the myopia of simply paying attention to structures of subjectivity that repeat and organize, sometimes for shorter, sometimes for longer, stretches of time. I believe that such myopia severely limits the scope of attention critical for the kind of therapeutic encounter psychoanalysis was created to sustain.

Acknowledging the above-mentioned limitation, I also recognize how an investigation of the socio-cultural influences on any psychoanalytic theorist/clinician can contextualize and enrich the significance of their contributions (see Kuchuck, 2014 for several examples). And so I begin this text with an attempt to reflect on how the ways in which I organize and interact within the contexts I find myself in have been impacted by my personal and social history. I am attempting to create an understanding for how this history might shape an approach to the theoretical and clinical narrations I have offered in this text for the practice of psychoanalysis. I am hoping that this brief set of reflections might assist you, the reader, to better make use of the chapters to follow, as you continue to consider and develop your own theoretical vision and practice. Following is my brief narration of this history.

My education in the significance of embodied rhythms began in a social context characterized by working-class values and practices. It was a challenging life I encountered as I began to walk and talk and play on the streets of Jersey City where, at age three, my best friend and I were set up as mini-gladiators, ringed by the older boys, to best the other in a fist fight. For what seemed like minutes we both refused. But egged on by his many brothers, my best little friend punched me in the face, drawing tears from me, cheers from the others. I quickly learned not to trust others and to strike first. I began to use a left-hook punch to knock my best friend to the floor and bloody his lip at every opportunity going forward. There were other acts of violence I committed in those "tender" days which shamefully I will not name, but which led my parents to move from that neighborhood to another quickly thereafter.

Nevertheless, I have painful memories of the two gangs on the street where I first played, neither of which would have little me, though I tried to be a member of both. I remember a slowly dawning recognition of differences between ethnic groups which often shaped safety or danger ... including Jews (of which I was one), Irish, Italians, Latinx, and African Americans. Sometimes it was not clear to me why I should fear those different from me. It was at this time that I first learned to attend to subtle embodied cues, such as a gaze averted to the ground, a stare held seconds too long, a facial expression of anger, a slight but quick movement of hand or foot, a pause in conversation, or increase in speech volume .... These and many more embodied signals, never given verbal articulation or time for reflection, became the rapidly appearing/disappearing signals of danger that I could use to achieve safety in such a socially complex and confusing world. These were lessons learned from emotional and physical trauma; a world in which I, like others around me, moved easily between roles of victim and perpetrator. In retrospect, as I reflect on my subsequent years of development, especially as I began to have the capacity to move around the city on my own volition, I became aware of the way that each city block in that town was a mini-community of socio-ethnic identity; some more, some less diverse, with significant consequences for safety or danger.

There was a clear dividing line on my street just one-and-a-half blocks east of the home in which I lived between ages eight and 18. It was Monticello Avenue, a dividing line marking neighborhoods of "whiteness" and "blackness." In my early teens, I crossed that avenue every school morning to attend Lincoln High School, where 70 percent of the student body shaped the daily rhythms of social activity out of their African American experience. I had been exposed to these social rhythms when I was born, and my mother's pregnancy left her bedridden for the first weeks of my life. Then, Mary Peace was as much involved in my maternal care as my biological mother. Mary lived on the other side of Monticello Avenue. She and her family, who often visited her and helped around our apartment during this time, were different in color of skin and speech rhythms. They were a source of care and learning for me. Later, I experienced the differences and similarities between the rhythms of my life and those of folks from that side of Monticello Avenue when our grammar school was racially integrated, and this continued through my high school years. These lessons in cultural difference emerged as drumming on the scarred wooden desks we sat at, … on the basketball team where embodied rhythms were central to failure or success, … on streets walking home in the dark where posture and gaze could draw unwanted attention or not, … and on the dance floor at social events where the doo-wop and soul music was that of Little Anthony and the Imperials, Smokey Robinson and the Miracles, The Marcels, or The Shirelles, and we danced the Twist, the Monkey, the Hucklebuck and the Mashed Potato.

I share this racialized dimension of my experience to indicate how it shaped the embodied rhythms I learned to attend to and enact at that time, and also to indicate that the intersection of race, as well as class, gender and religion at that time of my life happened with an impact for which I and others carried little reflective awareness, but often much confusion. In fact, I and so many others were quite unconscious of the economic and social arrangements of power and control which shaped our thoughts, actions and images of each other.

As I entered puberty, my attention was strongly drawn to jazz music which was part of the intellectual fervor of the artistic world happening across the river in the Bohemian enclaves of New York. I also soon realized that jazz was a unique artistic expression emerging from the convergence of musical practices coming from parts of Africa (particularly the field hollers of slaves emergent from work songs and ceremonial chants) and parts of Great Britain (particularly the tradition of balladry as stories sung). These traditions blended into what we now recognize and experience as "the blues" in its various expressions. I convinced my folks to buy me an alto saxophone and some lessons and I was off, having my first experience playing with classmates at a black church on Central Avenue in Jersey City. Soon after I became imbued with the avant-garde jazz movement, many of whose practitioners were based in the nearby East Village of New York City. Here again, unspoken embodied rhythms shaped experiences of acceptance/ rejection in this world of jazz which became my new social context of choice, catalyzing a lifelong process of deconstructing and recognizing the class and racialized stereotypes imprinted unconsciously by my neighborhoods of origin. It also was where I found my heroes, role models of integrity, perseverance and socially relevant creativity. During my late adolescence in New York and undergraduate years in Philadelphia I became an active, though uncelebrated, member of that artistic community, having great opportunities to know, study and/or play with some of the most influential practitioners of that period in jazz, particularly John Coltrane, Sunny Murray, Archie Shepp, Roswell Rudd, Byard Lancaster, and later in Philadelphia, Carl Grubbs. My sensitivity to embodied rhythms and the significance of these for experiences of power, safety and danger continued to develop in the context of these musical mentors.

Early career in community mental health

A significant element of the music I was playing was shaped by, and shaping, awareness of racial and class difference, and the structural arrangements driven by racism to sustain economic and political disadvantage for persons of color. I was influenced by several of my elders to find ways to become socially active to resist and transform such practices. I became an active member of the Community Involvement Council at The University of Pennsylvania and collaborating with the head of a local Boys Club and a local priest, I worked on neighborhood streets using sports and music to channel potential gang members into more constructive activities. These were white youth similar to many I had grown up among.

After graduation, I moved to New York City, still active in the music world, but where I also became part of a community mental-health team working in a single-room occupancy welfare hotel providing services to people who might otherwise return to psychiatric hospitalization or prison without the support of our team. It was then that I met Neil Altman who had recently returned from working in the Peace Corps in India and was working as part of a similar hotel project team. His work at integrating the unconscious and the social has been a continuing influence on me (Altman, 1995, in press). In both my work on the streets of Philadelphia and with those living in single-room occupancy hotels of New York City, my developing capacity to read embodied cues to help me grasp what otherwise might be invisible with regard to the suffering and/or desire of others, served to sharpen my capacity to recognize and navigate emotional turbulence as it emerged within or between persons.

My experiences in community mental health influenced me to seek a graduate education. After completing all requirements for my doctorate but the dissertation, I began to work with a group of young professionals who had come together out of concern for the epidemic of substance abuse, street gang and domestic violence, teen prostitution and child trafficking, etc. that was impacting youth suffering on the streets of New York City in the late 1960s and early 1970s. This group had met for several years to develop a new model bringing all services that a youth might need under one roof, creating a space, both physical and psychological, that did not repeat the alienating practices and physical environments associated with schools, clinics and even recreational and vocational programs at the time. Rather, The Door – A Center of Alternatives was a community-based model developed by this group as part of a project of The International Center for Integrative Studies, at that time an NGO of the United Nations, whose mission was to develop ways of thinking and acting, serving as alternatives to the alienating effects of specialization common to the first part of the 20th century. This specialization had created a silo effect, leaving disciplines, programs and departments disconnected, uncommunicative, unaware of, and thus unable to learn from and collaborate with, the activities of each other.

In contrast, The Door was a model of community in physical layout and interdisciplinary team service delivery. Physicians, nurses, nutritionists, psychiatrists, psychologists, social workers and other counselors, along with educators and artists, communicated together as a team structured in support of each youth attending The Door. Furthermore, this system of service delivery was nested in a 60,000 square foot physical context with 60-foot high ceilings and colorful service/activity areas laid out more like an open convention space than closed off separate floors with long hallways and offices with closed doors. In fact, at this location, the only closed off spaces were for medical examining rooms and offices containing confidential material.

I joined this group just at the point when the volunteer pilot project store-front phase had been completed. Now came the challenge, with a funded and large-enough space and staffing, to bring the total program vision into active expression. I worked at The Door for the next 13 years, helping to implement that mission and share it with others through supervision, training, workshops and consultations. For six years helping to administer, supervise and provide services as part of the Psychiatric Counseling Garden, and seven years serving as a consultant/trainer out of the Replication Unit, I worked with groups internationally, nationally, and locally to assist others in learning about the principles, systems, and strategies that we had developed at The Door. These strategies catalyzed our capacity to serve as many as 300 youths a day who would come to The Door space to use services and programs, all voluntarily. (I recently learned that The Door now serves around 600 youths a day.)

These strategies developed at and through The Door's community impact were the focus of initiatives I advanced to aid hundreds of groups and agencies worldwide. These clients were seeking, and continue to seek, to replicate the principles and systems developed at The Door in a way that responds to the unique needs of their local communities. My longest-term client, which in itself has become a unique model for reaching the underserved in a community, was El Puente, located in the Williamsburg section of Brooklyn, New York. At the time of writing, El Puente continues to grow in response to the needs of its community and serves not just the Latinx community in which it is based, but also residents of Puerto Rico through a satellite site on that island.

The basic strategy of The Door, then, was to shape a social and physical environment as a context for engaging the emotional suffering of the youth who would come to us daily, bringing the hope for opportunities to overcome their hardships and develop a more vital and constructive life. This was an opportunity for me to work with Door members (they were not called patients or clients) and colleagues, for understanding and addressing the unconscious sources of emotional suffering as part of a larger social context impacting vitality and agency. This was also a critical opportunity for me to experience how embodied rhythms occurring in the micro-moment dimensions of interaction with others were critically shaped by the social and physical environmental opportunities and constraints either facilitated or inhibited by such structural arrangements. More specifically, compartmentalized public housing space, associated with limited economic opportunity, often facilitated embodied shame and distrust fueled by emotionally overstimulating frustration and emotionally under-stimulating isolation and avoidance. Many of the youth upon first entering The Door environment, because of trauma and distrust coming from such environmental experience, found the verbal interview process threatening, thus making it difficult for staff to initially evaluate and facilitate the guidance of members to activities and services from which they might benefit. In such interactive fields, embodied rhythms spoke more loudly and clearly than words and could facilitate a sense of connection and recognition prerequisite to a sense of community membership and opportunity for finding one's unique and personal voice and direction.

At The Door, the center space functioned as an open town square facilitating embodied attention and sustained interest, fueled by emotionally calming interpersonal rhythms of pairs and groups interacting formally and informally in the open, thus creating a climate of safety and affiliation, of participation versus isolation. Developing and participating in these experiences as a staff member (all of whom were on the same first-name basis with members), provided me with more than a decade of experience, furthering my recognition of the significance of embodied interactive rhythms as adjunctive to, if not substitutive of, verbal interaction for effective clinical connection and community building.

Early training influences

In the last years of my work at The Door as a consultant/trainer, having completed my doctorate, I augmented my professional activities, returning to clinical work part-time in a local clinic. There I met and was supervised by James Fosshage who slowly introduced me to the post-Freudian trends emerging in psychoanalysis and particularly those concerning self psychology in which he was centrally involved. Through readings in his supervision group, I was exposed to Kohut's (1971) concept of empathy, a vision from Stolorow et al. (1987) of the intersubjective field of interaction, and the impact of micro-moment observations of infant/caregiver interactions by D. N. Stern (1985), and Beebe and D. N. Stern (1977) on psychoanalytic practice as these were being delineated in the work of Beebe and Lachmann (2002). I immediately found in Kohut's description of his attention to the vocal tone and rhythms of his patient Ms. F, in the attention to the interplay of subjectivities described in the clinical illustrations of intersubjectivity, and in the micro-moment rhythms and prosody of infant/caregiver interactions, parallels to my experience as a soloist and accompanist in jazz. Clearly these clinically focused concepts helped to explain my own early strategies of using attention to embodied rhythms as I navigated interpersonal vulnerability, safety and danger, and experiences of trauma described earlier. I soon found these concepts seminal to an integration in thinking and technique that I was developing in my own clinical work and writing. I presented these ideas as a coherent set of strategies with clinical illustrations in my first text, *The Musical Edge of Therapeutic Dialogue* (2000). Since the publication of that text in 2000 I have found my perspective and ways of working undergoing a continuous process of revision and development. This current text organizes and presents the evolution of this thought and way of working. Many of the chapters appeared in earlier drafts as published papers in psychoanalytic journals. They are presented here to reflect an unfolding coherence and focus leading to the most current vision I can bring to the challenges of this project.

Overview of chapters

And so the chapters of this text represent, in many ways, theoretical and clinical extensions and integrations of my early experiences, both personal and professional. The chapters unfold a continuing process of refining a way of attending to clinical interaction that both expands and focuses in on the interaction between emerging micro-dimensions of embodied rhythms and macro-culturally contextualizing meanings as they shape the capacities of both patient and analyst to bear and navigate the emotional experience of such interaction.

I begin Chapter 1 by addressing the limitations to the process of symbolization for communication in psychoanalytic work as the basis for an expansion/reformulation of clinical attention to include embodied experience as a source of unconscious meaning. The displacement effect of language and the futility that language meets, as description of lived experience, are key points recognized in the contributions of Daniel Stern and Jacques Lacan. This discussion is, then, augmented with a critique of assumptions underlying Freud's technique for analytic work, noting contributions from Irwin Hoffman which serve as a launching point for a relational approach to analytic attention expanded with an emphasis on micro-moment embodied communication in addition to symbolized communication. A clinical narrative is offered, highlighting the rhythms of movement between embodied and verbally symbolized communication as a basis for constructing emerging meanings, previously unconscious. The implications of this approach for expanding analytic attention to include registers of communication in addition to the verbal symbolic are then summarized.

With Chapter 2, I address the assumption of privileging stillness as a central strategy in the activity of the psychoanalyst. Is this the only effective clinical strategy for optimizing a psychoanalytic focus? I answer in the negative, emphasizing that stillness can have an array of potential affective impacts as opposed to the traditional assumption of neutral impact or the creation of a space for meaning to emerge. An example of the duration of silence is then offered to illustrate that attention to the polyrhythmic weave of micro-timing in the interactions constituted by analysand and analyst can prove to be at least as rich a fulcrum for generating meaning in the psychoanalytic process as a strategy of sustaining silence as space for transference projections by the analysand or reverie for the analyst. The impact of cultural practices and beliefs is then considered for how these can shape the scope and focus of analytic attention. In particular, the concept of attunement is revisited to demonstrate how a particular cultural perspective, which privileges a linear concept of time and timing, could fail to recognize the generation of subtle affective meanings from the polyrhythmic weave of timing, including matching and mismatching – a more complex and richer focus for analytic attention than just a moment of matching.

In Chapter 3, I address the challenge, complexity and uncertainty of finding language for *re-presenting* the fluidity of micro-moment patterning. The discussion, published in an earlier form as a response to comments by Cornell (2011) and Markman (2011) represents a rich exploration of the difficulties and possible strategies for managing the tension and paradox of this challenge. The discussion is also a model for respect and appreciation of difference.

Chapter 4 begins with a clinical narrative carefully illustrating a kind of attention to the fluid micro-patterning of polyrhythmic exchange described in previous chapters. Interaction dynamics, are brought into greater focus for their complexity and challenge to the analyst as these dynamics are shaped by cultural assumptions, practices and discourses. The analyst's vulnerability shaped by the limits of thinking, categorizing and recognition is illustrated and assisted with introduction of a non-linear dynamic model emphasizing the concept of *tipping point* as a useful, if temporary, categorical frame for such experience, otherwise quite complex, uncertain, and therefore difficult to narrate.

With Chapter 5, I continue to address the challenge of narrating the fluid dimensions of embodied rhythm by offering a renovation of field theory in psychoanalysis. I offer an elaboration for how to recognize and work with *fluid* registrations in addition to categorical and *structural* re-presentations of interaction conceptually and in clinical practice. A review of how Racker and Reis read Freud, augmented by previously unexamined aspects of Daniel Stern's conceptions of attunement and repeated interactions generalized (RIGS), builds toward a reformulation of how affect regulation might be better envisioned through the term *affect navigation* and its various meanings and uses. Clinical examples from clinician/theorists (including from my first book) representing relational and Bionion thought, illustrate how embodied registrations of rhythmic patterning, (which because of their fluidity cannot be re-presented symbolically/categorically), augment recognition of self-states and self-state shifts. Narration of fluid registrations, uncertain in their meaning, in addition to categorizing experience with culturally situated meaning, creates an expanded attention for the clinician to the unfolding and layering of her own emotional experience in addition to that of her patient. This further complexifying of experience in terms of the intersection of cultural lenses as introduced in the previous chapter is noted as a bridge to the next chapter.

Chapter 6 serves as a further extension of thinking initiated in the previous chapter. This chapter is built around a clinical encounter illustrative of the challenge/struggle for recognizing and working in terms of race. I employ perspectives and terms emerging from a vision developed by Frantz Fanon to represent issues of race for psychoanalytic practice that have begun to be recognized and discussed recently. These issues open up unprecedented challenges for theory and practice, particularly as they reveal the myopia of the terms and discourse with which we make meaning and practice clinically (see Altman, 1995; Holmes, 1992, 2016; Leary, 1997; Powell, 2018; Straker, 2004; Suchet, 2007; White, 2002; for a history of this recent attention). I examine the experience of my own need to perform in the role of rescuer, in tension with surrendering to the limits of an attempt at recognition within the discursive terms of a racist social order. In particular, I point to the limitations of verbal re-presentational categories/models in currently accepted psychoanalytic discourse as well as in the capacities of both analyst and patient to re-present complex, emotionally difficult to bear, racialized experience. I demonstrate the clinical value of expanding analytic attention to embodied registrations as one way of surrendering to this myopia of theory, and the effects of amnesia and/or erasure that racist discourse can have on re-presentations of traumatic histories for both patient and analyst.

With Chapter 7, I retrace key themes emerging in this and my first text. A shift in perspective *from edges to thresholds* is summarized to illustrate how clinical attention can expand from a vision of *states and state shifts* to include that of *continuous movement* where emotional turbulence is navigated within the polyrhythmic weave emerging as the clinical encounter. This navigation is made possible with the analyst's shifting attention between structural overlays and fluid micro-patterns of embodied experience for both interacting subjects. This vision is then made more complex and uncertain, and at the same time enriched, by the recognition of culturally contextualizing forces shaping discourses emerging from unconscious assumptions and practices reflecting a rich experience of intersectionality with race as a powerful force. Returning to the idea of communion as a building block of community, I posit that Jessica Benjamin's bonds of love involve the navigation of emotional turbulence within a social context that is either more or less facilitative of experiences of communion/community. Possibilities for communion are shaped or negated by the categories of discourse which valorize or abject, often on the basis of intersectional vertices of otherness. Given these complex dynamics, *bonds of discourse* (i.e. the categories with which we formulate and structure experience) are shaped by the bearability of emotional tensions flowing into and out of experiences of *recognition* and of *communion*. The story of psychoanalysis unfolds as the struggles for both practitioner and patient to navigate the challenge and uncertainty carried in the strain of these tensions.

Chapter 1

Body rhythms and the unconscious

Toward a reformulation of clinical attention with the polyrhythmic weave

This chapter introduces the limitations of symbolization, i.e. the displacement effect of language and the futility which language meets as it describes lived experience. As psychoanalysts involved in the "talking cure," how do we work with these limitations and still constitute therapeutic engagement with our patients? Using a clinical illustration based on the metaphoric value of jazz improvisation for attending to, and participating in, a psychoanalytic interaction (Knoblauch, 2000), I offer a strategy and a theoretical perspective. This perspective shares with those of La Barre (2001), Gentile (2007), Orbach (1999, 2003, 2004, 2006), Reis (2009), Sonntag (2006), Sletvold (2014) and others (Anderson, 1998; Anderson, 2008) a privileging of nonverbal embodied communication in a way that has rarely been demonstrated in clinical practice (see my discussion of precursors to our perspectives in Knoblauch (2000), Chapter 4, pp. 51–76.) The process of improvisation in jazz requires careful attention to nonverbal embodied dimensions of communication, particularly rhythm, tone and gesture, in order to recognize and express affect. A similar process occurs in the clinical exchange offering rich potential for recognition and expression when words are not being used or fail to express critical emotional experience – a condition particular to communication of unspeakable trauma.

Attention to *process* (I am here using the term "process" in a particular way to refer to the micro-polyrhythmic dimensions of the interactive exchange) was traditionally not given descriptive significance in narratives of clinical action. Rather, attention to *structures* of experience in the subjectivities of analysand and analyst has been the preferred metaphor for representation and explanation. The approach I am presenting expands analytic attention with particular focus given to process or how structured experience is "formed into." This is a dimension of meaning-making concomitant with communicative experience we semantically mark with terms such as symbolization or representation; information as delineated form. This expanded view offers a way to navigate the challenge of the limitations noted in my opening sentence, and to work with expressions of trauma about which analysands are not able to give verbal representation. This perspective incorporates embodied experience in addition to verbal symbolization as a portal into unconscious meaning and its centrality to therapeutic action.

From Freud through Stern and Lacan to Hoffman's relational thought and beyond

In his landmark contribution to understanding human development, Daniel Stern (1985) makes an observation resonant with the opening sentence of this chapter. He addresses the relationship between words and the experiences they are constructed to represent, explaining that,

> language is a double-edged sword. It ... makes some parts of our experience less shareable with ourselves and with others. It drives a wedge between two simultaneous forms of interpersonal experience: as it is lived and as it is verbally represented .... Language ... causes a split in the experience of the self. It ... moves relatedness onto the impersonal, abstract level intrinsic to language and away from the personal immediate level intrinsic to ... other domains of relatedness.
>
> (Stern, 1985, pp. 162–163)

Stern subsequently augmented this position incorporating a view that language can be part of a gestalt that is immediately grasped intuitively so that language can be abstract in its representational capacity but also an embodied lived experience for both speaker and listener (Boston Change Process Study Group, 2008).

Stern's point in 1985 was that what is lived is unable to be fully captured with its representation in words. This is a price we pay for constituting a mode whereby we can begin to both reflect on, and share experience, at least to some degree, with others.

Implicit to Stern's observation is the point that the operation of representing experience with word symbolization "permits the child [allows the adult] to begin to construct a narrative of his own life" (Stern, 1985, p. 162). But, it also becomes the form by which experience is split across different modes of relatedness. Speaking is a different register than what we feel. Lacan has addressed this phenomenon with more pessimism. He claims, "... the symbol manifests in itself first of all as the murder of the thing, and this death constitutes in the subject the externalization of his desire" (Lacan, 1977, p. 104). Stern addresses the cognitive aspect of the effect of symbolic representation. Lacan's point originally made about the effect of symbolization as an abstract representation of something lived and unable to be fully represented without important loss, has implications beyond just cognitive experience. Lacan's observation also concerns the effect of symbolic representation on affective experience. For Lacan, the splitting that Stern describes devitalizes or "murders" the thing represented. It reduces it to an object, which by its externalization can remove it from the immediacy of affective impact. Thus representation or symbolization constitutes a gap between what has been experienced and what is re-presented, a form of desire for that experience which has been lost. Lacan puts it this way:

> the subject is not simply mastering his privation by assuming it, ... he is raising his desire to a second power. For his action [*the symbolizing or objectifying of an experience with words*] destroys the object that it causes to appear and disappear in the anticipating provocation of its absence and its presence. His action thus negatives the field of forces of desire in order to become its own object to itself.
>
> (Lacan, 1977, p. 103, my addition in italics)

Another way to think about what Lacan says is to recognize that the symbolizing function of language memorializes an experience so that narrative can emerge. Narrative is requisite to memory, the process of representing an experience for storage and retrieval. But this form of memorialization, this process of representation, according to Lacan, requires a delimiting and delineating of experience such that it is *frozen in time*, deadened and devitalized as it is arbitrarily removed from the flow, process or polyrhythmic weave of continuous interactive experience. This splitting off and categorization of experience into a discrete non-continuous, symbolized "thing," creates two effects: (1) loss and (2) desire for that which one had experienced but is now lost, though capable of being "*remembered*," and only possibly re-experienced affectively, through the storage and retrieval functions that representation makes possible.

This understanding of how meaning is made possible for narration is central to Freud's method of the "talking cure." For it is attention to forms of condensation, displacement and substitution in the construction of narrated meaning that is the basis of the analytic method. Freud's evenly hovering attention emerged as the strategy for how the analyst could use herself to recognize, organize and respond to these particular structures of subjectivity in the patient's experience and begin to help the patient become conscious of experiences of loss and desire that were "repressed" when language was not available for remembering such experience. This process is given further consideration for its limitations concerning the relationship between repeating and remembering in Chapter 5. But for this discussion I focus on Freud's idea of trauma. Freud's conception of trauma is central to his approach to repression, as it was the affective unbearability of a particular experience, understood as an inability to manage libidinal energy, (i.e sublimate rather than discharge), that resulted in the splitting off of that experience not into a word but into some unconscious symptom. This understanding, in itself, presents an interesting problem, since symptoms were generally enacted or expressed somatically. Thus experience could either be sublimated through symbolization or enacted symptomatically. In either case a splitting occurred, either into a "*representation*" as word or a "*re-presentation*" as enacted or somaticized symptom.

Freud believed the talking cure of free association was a way to heal the splits caused by symbolization or symptomization. But, central to his idea of this process were two assumptions: (1) the capability of the analyst to attain a neutral and objective stance in providing interpretations, and (2) the capability of the analysand to attain an attitude where associations would be produced uncensored. When this became problematic, the analysand's difficulty was to be interpreted as defense. Hoffman (2006) has offered a compelling review of this second assumption building on his previous review (Hoffman, 1983) of the first assumption. In his landmark 1983 paper, Hoffman carefully demonstrates the impossibility of neutrality and therefore objectivity for an analyst through an examination of the subjective biases inherent in different theoretical stances characteristic of different psychoanalytic approaches to treatment. In his 2003 paper he expands his argument to include the subjectivity of the analysand as well as analyst. He convincingly demonstrates how clinically pivotal relational influences occur as a result of critical subjective coloring of experience on the part of both analytic participants. Building on Hoffman's contribution, I would agree with Mitchell's observation (Mitchell, 1977, pp. 13–14) that expectations for free association from the analysand or neutrality and objectivity from the analyst create unattainable ideals at best, if not illusions that could contribute to exceedingly brutal transferential or counter-transferential self-evaluations. Hoffman's perspective frees us from these persecutory expectations. Here, I want to add specificity to Hoffman's emphasis on relational dimensions of the transference/countertransference field to demonstrate how such specificity can expand analytic attention. First, let's consider the implications of his deconstruction of the free-association method.

Freud's method of free association is critically built upon the assumption of an ideal of purifying observation, of making it free of biases, feelings or other influences that could affect what comes to mind. Hoffman describes how this assumption is built on: "(1) the denial of the patient's agency, (2) the denial of the analyst's and the patient's interpersonal influence, and (3) the denial of the patient's share of responsibility for co-constructing the analytic relationship" (Hoffman, 3003, p. 2). Hoffman argues that in fact the personal involvement of the analyst, (compare this notion to the ideal of neutrality), leads to a different emphasis in therapeutic action that "amounts to a huge difference in terms of the kinds of experiences that are promoted and the likely basis for therapeutic action" (p. 12). He does not argue for the jettisoning of insight as central to change but rather, for "a climate that encourages both imaginative construction and critical reflection on the constructive process itself." He emphasizes, "Insight is embedded in a multifaceted relationship the whole of which offers a complex kind of corrective experience" (p. 14).

But if in relational analysis we focus, as Hoffman would have us do, on the ways in which what we enact with our patients can provide the material for reflection and further imaginative construction of meanings, the question remains, how are we doing this? If free association as a method contains the assumptions of attainability of ideal states that are not attainable, and so is questionable as the central, mutative method catalyzing therapeutic action in psychoanalysis, what, then, might be?

The norm that emerged for a relational method is to focus attention on what is enacted (see Aron, 1996; Bass, 2003, 2007; Black, 2003; Cooper, 2007; Davies, 1998, 2003, 2005; Hoffman, 1998; Jacobs, 1986, 1991; Ringstrom, 2001 for discussions), or created, not just by the patient, but by the patient and analyst in co-constructed patterns and meanings. As Hoffman illustrates in his work, reflecting on these enactments post hoc can lead to important therapeutic movement. In Hoffman's clinical illustrations as well as in those of several other relational analysts (see Bromberg, 1998; Cooper, 2003; Davies, 1998, Dimen, 2003, Harris, 1998, Lichtenberg et al., 2002, Mitchell, 1977), Ringstrom, 2001, D. B. Stern, 1997, for some illustrative examples), there has been a trend to develop meaning, that which, previously, has not been consciously articulated or recognized, out of attention not just to symbolic communication, but to what Hoffman has called non-interpretive interactions (Hoffman, 1998, pp. xiii–xvi, 182–183). In contrast to Hoffman's emphasis on this kind of attention and responsiveness as non-interpretive, Ogden (Ogden, 1994, pp. 108–110) has described these kinds of interactions as interpretive. He explains, "By 'interpretive action' (or 'interpretation-in-action') I mean the analyst's communication of his understanding of an aspect of the transference-countertransference to the analysand by means of activity other than that of verbal symbolization" (Ogden, 1994, p. 108). Here, I want to try to further unfold the implications of this trend and to give it more specific conceptual clarity for sharpening and expanding possibilities for analytic focus.

Freud saw association as a kind of repair or re-membering of a broken connection caused by repression. Repression would occur because of the unbearability of the affective meaning associated with whatever experience was repressed. Revisiting Freud today, we might wonder that repression is a problematic concept for trauma. I say that because our understanding of trauma has led us to recognize a major effect of trauma is that affective meaning does not get represented in words but rather split off in bodily symptoms. The split that Lacan and Stern describe is the effect of the trauma of using the word to create symbolic representation, not the effect of trauma resulting in embodied symptoms. The split pointed to by Lacan and Stern is central to Freud's method of free association in which the goal is a repair of this split. But this method fails to address the impact of trauma when words have not been created. It is difficult to reconnect a word to a thing when no word and no thing were ever recognized and symbolized. Attempts to do so often result in retraumatization. A close reading of Kohut's description of his difficulty with offering verbal interpretations to Ms. F gives us a vivid example of how this repetitive retraumatization occurs and can develop into an impasse. So, now we are talking about a different kind of split than Freud's method addresses: the split or gap caused by dissociation, what Kohut called the vertical split. This is a splitting off of experience on an affective register where affect is communicated and registered without the availability of word symbols. This recognition has led to significant pioneering work expanding analytic praxis to understand and conceptualize affect (see Spezzano (1993) and Stein, (1991)) and to account for and work with dissociative processes (see Bromberg (1998) and Davies and Frawley (1994)).

Building toward a relational "method," the innovative contributions of these clinicians and others have led to a number of revisions in understanding and approaching a patient's experience. Central to this work has been the placing of enactment as well as verbal association at the center of analytic attention. Here, as Hoffman emphasizes, insight is not jettisoned but part of the interactive experience that is promoted and the basis for therapeutic action. Thus, relational treatment, consistent with Kohut's intent following his insights about his work with Ms. F., shifts and expands the emphasis of analytic attention rather than replacing it. Within this expansion words are not just symbols, but also forms of action and thus enactment. Similarly, actions are not always, and just, acting out (Jacobs, 1986) but also ways in which patients communicate affectively and construct meaning in interaction with their analysts. So, if free association can be used to access affective meanings that are being communicated symbolically, how do we access what is being communicated through enactment but not symbolized with words?

Part of the difficulty is most of what is enacted falls under the radar of symbolization as Lacan and Stern observe. But, it is clear in reading the compelling clinical descriptions of those authors mentioned above and others that important and *different* kinds of attention are being paid to *different* experience other than just the semantic meaning of what is being communicated, and this activity is critical for analytic attention.

How can we talk about these differences? How can we describe and narrate this other form or these other forms of attention, these alternative foci to symbolizing activity? This challenge clearly contains a paradox because in order to describe the non-symbolic activity to which one attends, one needs to find a way of representing or symbolizing it with words. Stern would have us talk about lived versus symbolized experience. But, of course, we would still have to find a way to symbolize this lived experience in a way that would not repeat the problem of splitting off important registers that symbolization erases. Lacan, more pessimistic than Stern, would have us recognize the devitalizing effect of the word and how it constitutes the tension of desires – a gap between experience and its representation that is impossible to communicate and fully "know." (While I offer a response to this question in this chapter, I acknowledge and continue to further explore the unavoidable limitations to any such approach (see Chapter 3).)

Recent attempts by relational theorists and infant researchers have not closed this "gap" so much as having begun to attempt to explore what seems to be happening in the "gap." Bromberg has described this as *standing in the spaces*. Donnel Stern has described an attitude of curiosity that focuses the analyst on what is going on between patient and analyst but *unformulated*. The infant researcher Alan Fogel (1993) has distinguished between the *discrete state* and the *continuous process*. The cognitive researcher Wilma Bucci (1997) has distinguished symbolic from *subsymbolic* levels of activity. She explains that "The categorical function, by which the continuous gradients of perceptual experience are chunked into discrete prototypical images, is the core of the symbolizing process" (Bucci, p.142). In comparing subsymbolic with symbolic levels of cognitive processing, she explains,

> These [varieties of information processing] include representations and processes in which the elements are not discrete, organization is not categorical, processing occurs simultaneously in multiple parallel channels, high level units are not generated from discrete elements, and explicit processing rules cannot be identified.

She then points out,

> Subsymbolic processing accommodates infinitely fine variation; this processing is not represented by standard metric systems or computational rules. We recognize changes in the emotional states of others based on perception of subtle shifts in their facial expression or posture, and recognize changes in our own states based on somatic or kinesthetic experience.
>
> (Bucci, p. 194)

I would add to face and posture the subtle shifts in vocal tone, rhythm and turn-taking.

Fivaz-Depeursinge and Corboz-Warnery (1999), in their empirical study of family interactive patterns, find similar subsymbolic levels of processing to the cognitive levels as reported by Bucci. Family members:

> use multiple physical modalities in playing: their pelves, torsos, heads, gazes, facial expression, voice intonations, and gestures. Whereas these modalities come in 'packages' (for instance, leaning the torso forward, orienting the face 'enface' and greeting [Beebe & Stern, 1977; Cohn & Tronick, 1988; Weinberg & Tronick, 1994]), they also constitute distinct layers or levels .... Indeed, the partners can delineate different interactive domains with the pelves, torso, gazes and expressions.
>
> (1999, p. 58)

The Boston Change Process Study Group has called shared discrete states, *moments of meeting* and the activity in which such moments are embedded, a context of *implicit relational knowing*. Alexandra Harrison (2003) has described video research in child treatment illustrating a way that symbolized and non-symbolized events can be tracked and related, at least contiguously, as a basis for making subjective judgments about the co-constructing of affective experience and its significance for therapeutic action. I and my colleagues, Beebe et al. (2005) have reviewed eight models of intersubjectivity contributed in both the literatures of adult analytic treatment and infant research. We tracked differences in what was attended to as central to therapeutic change in the interactive process that is enacted. Attempting to integrate these different approaches in a treatment, Beebe has described her use of videotaping to focus on critical details of the implicit relational context and demonstrate how mutative activity occurred in treatment, at times, without symbolization. Using our own subjective and affective participation in treatment interaction, Ehrenberg (coming from an interpersonal perspective which she calls the intimate edge (1992)), Ogden (coming from an object relations perspective which he calls the primitive edge (1989)) and I, (coming from a relational perspective which I call the musical edge (2000)), each working with an intersubjective frame, have offered approaches whereby we expand our attention beyond the symbolizing process of free association to attend to other non-symbolized levels of activity where affective communication is occurring and meaning is being constructed. How can we better understand these new kinds of analytic attention and their implications for the kinds of non-interpretive interaction that Hoffman and others describe?

I believe that Bucci's observations in cognitive research, and those of Fogel and Fivaz-Depeursinge and Corboz-Warnery in infant/parent interaction, point to different registers of communicative experience. These registers of experience require new and different kinds of attentional strategies that can be useful in psychoanalytic practice. In response to this challenge, I offer a clinical example in which shifts in focus of attention can be tracked to illustrate the analyst's *rhythms of attention and attention to rhythms* emerging between symbolic communication and the processes of formation on acoustic and kinesthetic registers. Such attention can enrich the texturing of meaning constructed in analytic interaction. This attention can improve descriptions of what is happening in the "gap" between experience and its various registrations and representations that can constitute affective "gaps" (dissociations) between, as well as within, interacting subjects. I want to say more about the relationship between attention to structures of formation or information, and attention to a process in-formation. In order to ground these further observations with clinical illustration, consider this narrative of a particular analytic encounter between a patient, whom I will call Denise, and me.

Denise and me

As Denise flopped herself into the chair in front of me, her chest rose, filling with air, as much as she could take in. Then, when fully engorged, she suddenly and swiftly released the gas, with a deep grunt, ... no, growl. The trumpeter Rex Stewart would similarly punctuate the plaintive soundscape of an Ellington depression-era dirge. It was a cold damp January morning, dark and lonely with cloud cover obscuring the few hours of sunlight and relative warmth that we are sometimes allowed during these short days of deep winter. Often, and particularly recently, Denise had begun sessions with a similar intake and outflow of air, but the quality of her body resonance, the complex interaction of abdominal muscles, throat constriction and facial display had usually constructed a moan of despair. When Ornette Coleman's alto saxophone would moan similarly in the midst of his free-form jazz solos of the 1960s, I would experience a visceral resonance in the back of my head, gut and spine: a kind of internal downward spiral toward bottomlessness. Interestingly, I had never attended to Denise's moans with analytic curiosity until this morning. But now, I was impacted noticeably by this shift to a grunt. I was startled and moved in the way that I had been by Coleman's saxophone sounds. Denise was clearly different and her gesture cut a definite opening, a shift in my attention to her body and my body and the meanings that were being constructed kinesthetically.

My body? Well, before I could even begin to recognize the difference between now and then, or maybe, as the register in which recognition was first taking shape this morning, I found my gut swept with an indescribable sense that I can only call a soft sadness, a movement in muscles and hormones toward tears. But I did not begin to cry. Rather, I too took in a deep gutful of air. I sensed how it seemed to regulate my sadness, slow down the muscular constrictions and increasing skin temperature that accompanies the onset of tears. When I had filled to capacity, I released the breath, but with a different resonance, one of a deep quiet sound that came from the chest area and was somewhere between a moan and a sigh. Here our sound shapes briefly created an area of affective space; a space made possible (at this point out of our awarenesses) for something new to begin to emerge. We had co-constructed a pause in time, but one that immediately seemed to plummet in space as a parachutist out of a plane.

Then, just as rapidly, our eyes met. We exchanged brief nervous smiles. But the tension in the muscles of our faces clearly suggested this was not fun. I could feel it in my response and see it in hers. Now space was closing, as time shifted. The rhythms of our "eye dialogue" here were quick and nervous, starting and stopping like the twists and turns that Bartok would command in his compositions, or Cecil Taylor would explode in his piano improvisations. These syncopations, combined with our earlier sound shapes, constructed feelings of uncertainty and hypervigilance.

Denise, often depleted and hopeless in these states of uncertainty and hypervigilance, would speak of her sense of failure and inability to feel as if she were measuring up to anything in her professional growth and personal life. She could find no satisfaction, no vitality in anything – not in her relations with her colleagues, not in her accomplishments, not in her intimate life. Nothing mattered. And yet, she could see how others would tell her that she was performing effectively in her job, or that sex was satisfying and she and her lover were getting along well and fighting with more fairness as compared to earlier in their relationship. But no, nothing was good enough.

I noted that Denise seemed hopeless as before, but now rather than depleted, as we began to speak, her tone was strengthening and her rhythmic forward pressing flow, felt full with anger; a different affective texture for our context. Was hopelessness shifting to hope on some unformulated level of experience (D. B. Stern, 1997)? I couldn't tell at this point. I wondered about her satisfaction with me and the treatment, her inability to find anything good enough in what we were doing, in how responsive or not I had been/was being to her. I noted the parallel meanings to her life descriptions and our work, our relationship. She replied, slightly shifting to sadness but then regaining the forward movement of her anger, that yes, she was unhappy with what we were doing, or maybe not doing. Then, ambivalently she began to shift again. Yes we had been making some progress. There were those sessions in which we seemed to get very close and deep, in which she felt maybe for a brief moment or two that I was getting her, that she was feeling gotten. We had explored these moments when they occurred earlier, and found them to be shot through with erotic and destructive feelings, constructing a kind of mutual devouring, mutually engorging emotional experience of each other. As part of this experience, Denise noted that our week of sessions seemed to have a rhythm marked by a dissociated, devitalizing start which then moved toward a last-session-of-the-week climax, fraught with complex somatic and semantic encounters, stimulating, if not overstimulating, but never enough – only to be drained of feeling and meaning into some dissociated space again by the beginning of the next week.

I had wondered with her in the past about how much she was experiencing me transferentially as some version or versions of her father, to whom she had been very close and whose death had only exponentially potentiated her eating disorder and self-mutilating, which took her through a series of hospitalizations. Maybe in the weekly rhythm we were re-enacting the loss of her father resonated by the death of my affective responsiveness to her, as recreated in the unfolding affective patterning, consisting of the unbearable sense of her inability to continue to vitalize him or me for which she either punished herself as previously recreated in her starving and bleeding, or dissociated.

While her previous treatments had been a path back to relative satisfaction and relatedness, as she pursued a somewhat successful athletic career and then higher education for the current professional activity in which she was clearly excelling and developing status and recognition, nothing had ever been enough. She could never hold onto, in fact, even ever feel, a sense of fulfillment, of having enough. It was never enough. Nothing could ever be enough. We both sat in the silence of the long pause of despair that this emptiness, this absence of presence had created between and within us. Again, we were constructing, though with significant pain, a space-expanding time warp, an opening for some new melody or syncopation to come forth and begin to constitute a new meaning between us.

Suddenly it occurred to me that either I had never asked about or had dissociated the time in her development when her eating disorder and self-mutilation had begun. We had always focused on the difficulty she had accepting the death of her father and never attempted to wonder about the fact that her difficulties had begun much earlier in life, as I now began to remember. My question was tentative, but clear. Denise responded to my query with a shift in body, rhythm and tone. Her face and posture relaxed. Her tone shifted from the punishing whine of adolescent anger to a lower register of sophisticated curiosity and collaboration. She began to recall how close she had been with Dad as a child. In fact, she had almost been his little boy. They had done so much athletically together. She would do things with him like biking, swimming, mountain climbing and running. She became her father's number-one companion in these activities with which they both filled themselves as much as possible.

But, now she remembered. It was when she began to grow breasts and her body shifted from that hermaphroditic phase that can be achieved in pre-puberty but rarely sustained with the onset of menses that she began to despair and self-destruct. I wondered whether her enacted symptoms were not a crying out into the world by the "boy" companion she had been to her father and longed to be forever, of that young "boy's" sense of annihilation. That self-version of Denise was disappearing and would be extinguished by her awful body which refused to obey her desire. The only thing to do was to punish her body, and so she did.

Her eyes widened and her voice shifted to a rhythmic vitality which I could recognize from the past, but never really see and hear as I was hearing now – the voice of that young boy, that subjective experience of being father's special companion that had been sequestered to the ghost realms by the curse of genetic physiology and against which Denise had battled with alcohol, drugs, food and blade to no avail. Now we could be two close collaborating companions.

Denise spoke more of her relationship with her father, of how wonderful those days were, and of how her father withdrew from her after puberty. It was as if their relationship had died. My body was suddenly filled with a different set of sensations than I was used to in responding to Denise. Previously, such emotional closeness had catalyzed powerful feelings of erotic desire or strange dystonic feelings of aggressiveness or fear. We had spoken about an early childhood experience she had had with boys in which they would play a game of holding someone's head under water until that person was almost close to drowning and then at the last minute letting him up for air. I think I had sometimes felt as if she were pushing my head under water, forcing me into confusion and self-doubt as to whether or how I could ever be good enough for her as an analyst. As we talked about this, she noted that she had similar feelings as a patient, as you would expect in line with the self-doubt and denigrating feelings with which she was constantly haunted. We had observed how much analysis could feel at times to both of us as if we were masochistically holding our heads under water too long. Now, as I write this narrative, I can see how we constructed a sadomasochistic pattern when we found ourselves repeatedly enacting, in our interaction, the dynamics of her internal struggle with her sequestered "boy" self whom she unconsciously rarely allowed up for air, but whose presence kept popping up in the rhythms and tones between us until now, when I finally could recognize and name him, and begin to sense what it might have felt like to be him.

This shift into vital lively rhythm and tone was suddenly perturbated again. Was Denise about to hold my head under? Her verbal stream had decelerated. The boyish enthusiasm had left her face and voice. But now there was something touchingly little-girlish and sad in her expression, and her voice came from the throat constrictions that construct higher frequencies, the tonal realm of childhood discourse – again a different version of self. She looked directly into my eyes, her eyes wide with wonder and questioning. She noted that when she thinks of her father in her reveries, it is not the lively companion of her "boyhood." But, rather, she sees the dying father gasping for his last breath on his hospital bed. As she spoke, my body filled with feelings that were not erotic, aggressive or fearful. Rather, I found myself, now unable to use breath to regulate my sadness. A deep and initially indecipherable grief flowed up from within. Then, I experienced a brief internal memory fragment of my father lying in his death as I viewed him before his funeral. My eyes began to fill with tears. Sensing this palpable shift in me, Denise queried, "What's the matter?" There was a tender tone of motherly comfort in the delivery and flow of her utterance suggesting still another self-state. I wondered if her inability to hold onto feelings of satisfaction with and relatedness to her achievements, colleagues, partner and me were not colored by the unconscious and, until this moment, dissociated internal tie with her dead father. Stunned, she dropped her gaze to the floor, attempting to self-regulate. She looked up to say she never had considered this, but that it felt true. This time her voice shifted from a soft maternality, to a deeper firmer strength – should I risk saying, paternality? But, no, this was a different sense of authority or agency than Lacan would attribute to the paternal. Rather, this voice seemed to combine the resonance of a child's wonder, a mother's capacity to hold and absorb, and a father's capacity for delineation. In fact, these generational and gender-stereotypic distinctions fail to discretely capture what more accurately seemed to wash and blur in the unparsed continuous sense of her hermaphroditic voice and body as I sat in my chair still trying to regulate my own flow of teary awe at the depth of connection and companionship that was momentarily filling our space together. Maybe for a moment we were both vulnerable little boys. Or maybe we were just both vulnerable in a heightened momentary flowing sense of self and other and loss, unfettered by discrete categorical distinctions of gender or age.

I close this description still wondering about how this unfolding patterning of tone and rhythm on kinesthetic and affective edges of shifting self-states affected my own countertransferentially dissociated potential for multiplicity, of how much I was experiencing my mournful little boy crying with the little boy/girl whose loving father had also died and who couldn't be a little boy anymore, at the same time that I was holding a soft, safe place in time and space, at the same time that I was recognizing, reflecting and delineating in words the significance of the internal presences of an annihilated little boy/girl and dead father which had become black holes of emptiness in Denise's self-experience. In subsequent sessions Denise has begun to talk more about how "masculine" she feels and how confusing it is as she feels good about herself in this way but also feels that others become threatened or upset if she does not hide this aspect of herself.

Discussion

In the opening comments of this chapter I emphasized that relational treatment shifts, and I now would add expands, the scope of analytic attention rather than replacing it. Let's look at the different attentional foci that I employed in my narrative of the clinical sequence with Denise and how these interacted in the process of forming meaning. I will briefly review 31 points of foci for attention occurring in both symbolic and non-symbolic registers, three of which marked nodal points where the registers intermingled to construct meaning. Note here that I am using the term nodal point to designate a moment in which attention to non-symbolic communication facilitates a symbolic representation of affective experience.

But first, an important cautionary note. This highly discrete, symbolic analysis constructed post hoc, should not be taken as a model or prescription for analytic attention. Rather, it is a writing practice, an exercise in reflection which can allow us to consider previous processes which occurred often without reflection or verbal articulation. While many of the events I have selected for attention were conscious and intentional on the part of the analyst or analysand, the important point to be illustrated is the way in which spontaneously improvised, unconsciously enacted phenomena, at times, can be recognized and responded to for their mutative potential as they interweave with reflected upon activity in psychoanalytic interactions.

Point #1 occurs as Denise growls – a non-symbolic registration. Point #2 occurs as I experience a soft sadness in my gut – a non-symbolic registration. Point #3 occurs as I release breath between a moan and a sigh – a non-symbolic registration. Point #4 occurs with the exchange of our eyes and nervous smiles – a non-symbolic registration. Point #5 occurs as I reflect on Denise's pattern of negating her thoughts and actions, "nothing was good enough" – a symbolic registration. Point #6 occurs as Denise's tone and rhythm strengthen – a non-symbolic registration. Point #7 occurs when I articulate the parallel between her hopelessness in herself and in me – a symbolic registration in response to her non-symbolic registration. This is the first of three nodal points.

Point #8 occurs as Denise reflects on her anger and our work – a symbolic registration. Point #9 occurs as we sit in the silence of despair over Denise's never feeling fulfilled – a non-symbolic registration. Point #10 occurs when I reflect in reverie that I had never inquired about the time her eating disorder began – a symbolic registration. Point #11 occurs when I give this question verbal articulation for Denise – a symbolic registration. Point #12 occurs as Denise's tone shifts from an adolescent whine to a lower register – a non-symbolic registration. Point #13 occurs as Denise recalls her closeness with her father – a symbolic registration. Point #14 occurs when Denise's voice shifts to the rhythmic vitality of a young boy – a non-symbolic registration. Point #15 occurs when I reflect in reverie that we could be two close companions – a symbolic registration. Point #16 occurs when Denise reflects how the relationship with her father "died" at the onset of her puberty – a symbolic registration. Point #17 occurs when I feel my body respond with vitality to Denise's reflection – a non-symbolic registration. Point #18 occurs as we revisit in words her early childhood experience of holding another's head under water – a symbolic registration. Point #19 occurs as we articulate in words the similarity between the feeling of her early childhood experience and what we do to each other in treatment – a symbolic registration. Point #20 occurs as I reflect in post hoc reverie on the possible transferential and countertransferential meanings of her childhood experience as the sadomasochistic dynamics of that experience are reenacted in treatment – a symbolic registration. This is the second nodal point marking the culmination of transducing the non-symbolic registrations of Denise's impact on me and my impact on her into transferential and countertransferential symbolization.

Point #21 occurs as Denise's verbal stream decelerates and her tone shifts to childlike high frequencies – a non-symbolic registration. Point #22 occurs as Denise articulates with words the shift in her reverie from her "boyhood companion" father to her dying father – a symbolic registration. Point #23 occurs as I find myself unable to regulate my feeling of sadness with breath – a non-symbolic registration. Point #24 occurs as I experience a memory of viewing my father just prior to his funeral – a symbolic registration. Point #25 occurs as my eyes fill with tears – a non-symbolic registration. Point #26 occurs as Denise enquires about my state – a symbolic registration. Point #27 occurs simultaneous to #26 in which I sense the maternal tone of Denise's utterance – a non-symbolic registration. Point #28 occurs as I suggest that Denise's feelings of not being good enough are related to an unconscious and, until this moment, dissociated tie with her dead father – a symbolic registration. Point #29 occurs as Denise, stunned, drops her gaze to the floor, clearly attempting to self-regulate – a non-symbolic registration. Point #30 occurs as Denise confirms my interpretation – a symbolic registration. Point #31 occurs simultaneous to #30 in which I sense the tone of Denise's voice to combine a kind of hermaphroditic synthesis in voice and body – a non-symbolic registration. This is the third nodal point marking a culmination intermingling symbolic and non-symbolic registrations, a recognition of this polyrhythmic weave, a process forming into a structured point of interpretation and a shift in Denise's capacity to symbolize her internal experience and to regulate and express her grief.

With this analysis, I have tracked 16 points of non-symbolic registration and 15 points of symbolic registration. It would be interesting to analyze the clinical narratives of those reporting on the impact of symbolic associations or those who include descriptions of enactments. I would guess that the first group would reveal a scarcity of attention to non-symbolic registrations, overlooking the significant, in-process micro-moment forming-into of meaning occurring with those registrations. I would guess that the second group would be impacted by non-symbolic registrations, but rarely reporting the bi-directional influence of these registrations and their pivotal impact on mutative moments in treatment. I would guess this because enactments are only infrequently attended to with descriptions of micro-moment detail where in-process construction of meaning is being carried along affectively significant registers of voice and body movement.

At points in an analysis where the patient brings an analyst to the edge of what might be comprehended or communicated with words, indications of meaning are often being communicated in embodied registers of experience. At such points, the analyst is often affectively flooded or anesthetized, confused, if not uncertain and/or caught in a frozen moment of fright. Attempts to regain psychic equilibrium for the analyst's self-regulation/organization can be facilitated by the kind of expanded focus that includes non-symbolic embodied registrations of experience/communication. But, at this point in the discussion I want to use the post hoc perspective made possible in this writing exercise to think about how an analyst's attention comes to include any particular dimension of the clinical exchange, symbolic or otherwise. I do this with a consideration of the theory or metaphor of mind implicit to the analyst's scope of attention. How an analyst conceptualizes mind is central to how an analyst represents her own or her analysand's subjective experience. This is the particular discourse an analyst employs. The capacity of an analyst to represent in narrative the impact of particular dimensions of subjective experience (both structural and process dimensions) can contribute significantly to the delineation of the scope and boundary of what is cognitively recognizable and/or affectively bearable at any moment in a particular analysis for both analyst and analysand. What is not represented or unbearable is often dissociated. What is not represented could also go unrecognized because the terms of discourse cannot adequately re-present what constitutes particular moments of experience. With this in mind, I have offered three ways with which mind can be conceptualized, each of which has been associated with particular clinical approaches. We can see the potential of each of these conceptualizations for creating particular openings in the clinical activity in my encounter with Denise.

First, let's consider a conceptualization of mind I have called the hydraulic model of mind (Knoblauch, 2000, pp.91), a kind of algebraic metaphor in which a finite amount of libidinal energy is distributed within a closed system of three structures. Too much energy in any place in this closed system can be experienced as unbearable, causing structural fragmentation as in the kind of ego splitting earlier described by Freud and further elaborated by Fairbairn (1958) and Kohut (1971).

This conceptualization of internal splitting effectively captures the way that neither Denise nor I would be able to hold onto the intensity of the erotic sadomasochistic exchanges that would characterize the final sessions of our weekly meetings, when we would begin the following Monday. Rather, Denise described the initial moments of our encounter in the first weekly session as devitalized and dead. This conceptualization then helps to organize how dissociation can disorganize/reorganize both reflective and affective registrations of experience. Our encounter was once again given breath and rhythm with the emergence of a focus of attention on our embodied experiences that shaped the present moments unfolding in the new week. For both of us, in the opening moments of each set of weekly sessions, feelings of aliveness and connectedness to our own embodied experience, as well as to the other's, were unavailable, and conceptualized as fragments split off from awareness.

A second conceptualization recognizes organizations of identifications and counter-identifications, complementary and concordant (Racker, 1968), volleying back and forth between patient and analyst which can precipitate transference/countertransference enactments. This metaphor constitutes an elaboration of the hydraulic mind. With such a representation, the scope of analytic attention is expanded to recognize the interaction between two subjectivities to be the field within which mind is being constituted. (This is a view developed by the various intersubjectivity theorists writing over the past two decades. See our work acknowledging these contributions, (Beebe, Knoblauch, Rustin & Sorter, 2005, pp. 2–3).) This view is further augmented with the recognition that subjectivities are always constituted within cultural contexts, often multiple and complex in their impact such that the subjective experience of having a mind is always constructed within, and constricted by a network of shared beliefs and practices. This contextual cultural matrix makes certain kinds of experiences visible and certain kinds of experiences invisible on the basis of a hierarchy of power gradients of value. Mind differentiates into an increasingly complex kaleidoscope (Davies, 1998) of possible patterning. I have called this the plastic model of mind, a kind of geometric metaphor in which an increasing number of systemic arrangements of representations with affective valence are emerging out of the experience of interaction with others (Knoblauch, 2000, p. 92).

This conceptualization of kaleidoscopic patterning shaped within a field of intersubjective experience captures the way that Denise and I eventually came to recognize how we constituted a particular enactment of the traumatizing loss of mutual recognition and desire as experienced with her father, in the patterning across our weekly rhythms of interaction. Once we were able to recognize this patterning we could begin to reflect further about past and present patterns as meanings were emerging and remerging in the rhythms of our interaction.

It is just this subtle and difficult-to-represent fluidity of interaction on which meaning is in-formation that constitutes a third way to conceptualize mind. This is not a model of a space or place, but rather a model of movement and interactivity. We can speak of **minding** or giving attention to the polyrhythmic weave on embodied (acoustic and kinesthetic) dimensions of the interaction from which faintly sensed meanings are not yet emergent, but possibly beginning to gain a degree of representation, not yet fully symbolized. Donnel Stern has described this as *unformulated experience* (Stern, 1997). With this model, minding is a lively interactive process not a structure. I have called this process a resonant model of minding, a kind of calculus or algorithmic metaphor, a sense of movement in attention that shapes the conceptualizing process, a movement that happens in the gaps between, and accounts for the breakdown and coalescence of the experience of discrete symbolic representations as structure (Knoblauch, 2000, p. 95).

This conceptualization of a process of minding can provide analyst and analysand with a compass for navigating the uncertain and sometimes frightening interacting currents constituting the fluidity of meaning that is still in-formation and not yet structured. It is an experience of resonance, an embodied dimension of the interaction within which faintly sensed indications of meaning come as form, intensity and timing (see Trevarthen (1993, p. 126) and Jaffe et al. (2001)). Attention to these dimensions – what Bucci calls the subsymbolic and I am here calling the non-symbolic – were the indications from which Denise and I were able to create articulation for particular self-states of varying affective bearability and give eventual symbolic meaning to our experience. For example, the emergence of the adolescent self, the childlike self, the maternal-like self and the paternal-like self, were each heralded by a shifting patterning in voice tone and rhythm, facial expression, eye focus, or body movement. Attention to these registrations opened up the opportunity for recognition and reflection, thus enriching the meaning-making exchanges occurring in a symbolic register for both of us. Note that such recognition of registration was sometimes bi-directional and sometimes self-reflective, as both Denise and I attended to different registrations in ourselves and each other.

The polyrhythmic weave of movement back and forth between symbolic and non-symbolic registers (as well as within and across embodied modalities) allowed for the construction of more finely tuned and complexly intertwined meanings for different discrete states experienced subjectively by analyst and analysand, initially emerging as, or coming into, a recognizable and representable form out of the flow of affective currents generated intersubjectively. This made possible nodal point 1, in which I was able to interpret the resonance between Denise's pattern of recurring hopelessness throughout her life experience and now within our relational patterning. With nodal point 2 I was able to articulate our previously enacted transferential/countertransferential sadomasochistic patterning, which was the way that hopelessness was sustained in our relating for further attention and generation of meaning. And with nodal point 3, Denise and I were both able to symbolize and affectively experience the splitting off of a loving tie between father and child to protect against the pain of grief which Denise was then able to begin to feel and express; and finally how much the meaning of that loss had to do with Denise's gender spectrum of self-experience, which, as reflected in the rhythms and meanings of the session's weave, were constricted by conflict and ambivalence over expressing certain forms of strength.

Nodal point 3 demonstrates a critical benefit that a resonant minding scope of attention can afford. Working with this particular conceptual lens can help the analyst to expect the kind of uncertainty, multiplicity and vulnerability that can trigger self-protective moves by the analyst, experiences of victimization leading to retreat and/or retaliation, or in the most unbearable moments, dissociation. Attention to embodied experience of one's own, or of another, provides the analyst not with a theoretical life preserver, but rather an expanded navigational strategy for negotiating the complexity and blind spots of the psychoanalytic interaction. Such a strategy involves attention to often subtly registered signals, enacted communications in the analytic exchange, which can help the analyst in her struggle to regain equilibrium and focus in the face of disequilibrating experience and loss of cognitive organizational capacity. Feelings in one's gut, muscular constricting or collapse, facial configurations, melodic or syncopated dimensions of speech flow and or hand or foot movement, i.e. pauses, punctuations or cross-modal "phrasing" in concert with other embodied cues construct intuitive bridges across the gaps within and between subjectivities. For the analyst, these intuitive bridges become important registrations of experience in the face of vulnerability, struggle and bearing the affective weight of not knowing. In my moment-to-moment struggle to bear the hopelessness that Denise frequently brought me in touch with, both concerning her experience of her life and our experiences of the analysis, attention to registrations in Denise's body from her groans and growl, to her eye movement, to her vocal tonal/rhythmic shifts, and also to registrations in my body, including muscular constrictions, the rhythms of my visual and vocal activity in interaction with Denise, as well as my tearing up, helped me to navigate and work with Denise to create more nuanced meanings out of the powerful symbolic and non-symbolic weave that we constituted.

These points of consideration contribute to an emphasis on the significance of expanded forms of analytic attention as a way to elaborate our narrations of what is happening in the "gaps" that emerge in our work. While these gaps can ultimately never be closed, the approach I am illustrating in this chapter emphasizes attention to subtle embodied micro-exchanges occurring in any analytic interaction as a way to expand our participation and reflection. This expansion in analytic attention can make possible a broader and richer range of meaning and affect available for both analyst and patient to construct and inhabit.

Chapter 2

Conceptualizing attunement within the polyrhythmic weave

The psychoanalytic samba

Central to psychoanalysis as Freud conceived it has been the use of silence. Within this conception, silence is understood to create an opening for the analysand to fill with symbolic images from dreams, slips of the tongue, or associations, each of which could carry significant unconscious meaning. Silence is the strategy for creating an ambience of objective neutrality, metaphorically: a blank screen upon which the analysand will transfer meanings in various symbolic forms. The analyst's stillness provides a unique opportunity for the analysand to have these transference experiences with the analyst. These experiences are understood to illuminate ways that the analysand experiences and relates to others. The analyst's stillness has also been considered for the ways it can facilitate the analyst's attention to a reverie process potentially rich in meanings understood as generated in the analytic interaction (see Cooper, 2008, pp. 1045–1073; Freud, 1912, p. 112; Ogden, 1997, p. 588).

The question of timing is raised in this tradition (Glover, 1931/1955) with regard to when in response to the analysand's verbal productions the analyst should break stillness and formulate a verbal interpretation. Considerations of timing with regard to the effects of silence, such as duration and the potential contextual meanings of silence, particularly the effect of silence as a non-neutral communication of affect, are not within the scope of such a conceptualization. In other words, within this conceptualization, major emphasis is placed on the timing and form of the analyst's verbal interpretations as a way to optimize a just-right intensity and focus for a mutative impact for the analysand. The analyst's embodied presence in the space and time between such optimal verbal interventions is conceptualized as best managed with strategies for neutrality, which would reduce, if not erase, any impact and meaning for the analysand.

On the other hand, researchers of infant/caregiver interaction interested in psychoanalysis have investigated the complexities of timing and the many possible meanings that variations in timing could construct as one organizes experience within the flow of clinical interaction. These researchers have used observations of human interaction registered with videotape (see Beebe, 2005; Downing, 2004, 2008; D. N. Stern, 1985, 2004 for some examples), bringing attention to the significance of micro-moment exchanges for the construction of meaning in the performance of clinical observation and intervention. Within the polyrhythmic weave, we can attend to the ways that pauses in speech flow, while representing an absence of talking can have a variety of meanings. Additionally, rhythmic accents in speech or other embodied dimensions of communicative exchange can carry affectively powerful meanings. La Barre (2001, 2005) and I (Knoblauch, 2000, 2005, 2008) offer illustrations emphasizing the role of embodied rhythmic patterning to the creation of affectively significant meaning in clinical interaction (also see relevant research describing infant–caregiver interaction, including Feldman et al., 1996; Jaffe et al., 2001; Lewis & Goldberg, 1969; D. N. Stern et al., 1977; Stern & Gibbon, 1979).

Here, I am extending the above reflections about the weave of two registers for meaning-making: polyrhythmic embodied and symbolic. I extend my thinking with considerations for how these different registrations of meaning are often shaped in the subjectivity of the listener or speaker, in part, by cultural beliefs and practices for both analyst and analysand that might be similar or different. These beliefs and practices, often unreflected upon as part of the psychoanalytic process, contextualize subjective experience in addition to the intersubjective dynamics of the dyad within any present moment. For example, in addition to the possibility of creating a sense of abandonment or, on the other hand, a space for reflection, a pause might be considered in other ways than by what is absent. Central to this consideration is the recognition that absence can be experienced or dissociated, as it is constituted within an interaction between a subject and her context, both dyadic and cultural. Cultural lenses can focus or foreclose *the ways available for thinking about and organizing such meaning.* While such cultural lenses can be effected with the discursive rules of exchange, i.e. what is made visible or hidden within word definitions, cognition (reflection and meaning-making) and affect are also impacted by non-worded embodied registrations. This is a central consideration to critical thinking about the pragmatics of theoretical frames used by the analyst for clinical judgment and action. So here I am specifically examining the question of what might be filling the interval in a particular clinical moment by attending to non-symbolic dimensions of interactive activity and their significance for creating meaning. I am additionally interested in beginning to weave into such considerations the way that the analyst's experience is shaped by different cultural lenses.

Clinical narration of a pause considered in context

Moments … … … really … … just … … short … … bundles … … of … … seconds … … seem … … to … … str … … tech … … long stre … … tches whose duration seems so great in contrast to the minutes marked by the clock on the table by my chair. These clock minutes seem to pass in rapid cadence when the patient I will call Warren and I are engaged in the kind of animated dialogue that can easily characterize the greater part of any analytic session we have. (Warren is a high-powered executive. He presses forward. He can do a lot more in his time than most of his peers can accomplish in their time.) But now, Warren's facial display shifts suddenly and severely. From a kind of mask-like-optimistic-gets-it-done-kind-of-guy smile, the tips of his mouth, slightly turned up, now collapse. (You can feel this in your face if you just mock up a smile and then let it go. Let it flop. Your entire lower facial display around your mouth just drops. Try it.)

This salient signal, flaring into my attention as I sit opposite Warren, is setting off seismic shifts in me, between us and (I infer) in Warren. My gut is filled with a sense of free fall away from the frenetic fantasies of efficiency and responsiveness that shape the timelines of my patient's days and that have been, and are even now, programming the patterning of our clinical interaction and, particularly, my countertransferential sense of who I feel pressed by Warren to be with him. Warren feels the need to be "on it" all the time. He reminds me of what I consider a distorted sense of empathic responsiveness or what, in the past, adopting a word twist from the Stolorow group, I have called *immaculate attunement*. This use of attunement is unidirectional and has been characterized by Beebe as hypervigilant, hypertherapeutic, hypertracking. Jaffe, Beebe and their coworkers offer a bidirectional alternative that characterizes a more sophisticated understanding of what attunement can feel like. They observe *level of activity* as a co-constructed interactive patterning more pervasively constituting dialogic rhythmic coupling than simply matching of tempo (Jaffe et al., 2001). This conception is quite close to a similar description offered by Seligman in an unpublished paper (Seligman, 1990). Both the Jaffe group and Seligman observing infant–adult interaction, emphasize the nonperiodicity of such rhythmic coordination. Here, coordination is a larger unit constituting a "wider ecology" (Jaffe et al., 2001, p. 89) to the context-sensitive complex layering of dialogic rhythms. These rhythms often occur in nonlinear patterning of different time scales and, like all unconscious phenomena, are only available for observation and organization as a tip of the iceberg, a metaphor that I will begin to rework later in this chapter. This distinction, while possibly appearing clear, is complex and difficult to give precise definition. I will continue to address this distinction in different theoretical and clinical contexts throughout this text. My intent is to engage this distinction in these differing contexts as an effective strategy for overcoming problems with precise definition by offering a variety of descriptions which can overlap but also augment each other, thus enriching understanding while not denying the limits of description.

Returning to Warren and me, I realize that until this micro-moment shift that we are constituting, I too have been feeling pressure to be *immaculately attuned*. The problem with this superego expectation, and the reason it is a distorted sense of empathic responsiveness, is first, that a nonstop attention to the states of others is physiologically not possible given the limits of human perception, and second, that a too tightly entrained tracking and responsiveness to an other has been associated with the creation of insecure patterns of attachment (see Beebe's work on attachment and responsiveness in infant–caregiver dyads, which emphasizes a midrange of responsiveness characterizing secure attachment bonds between infants and mothers). In other words, such close tracking would be clinically contraindicated for optimizing patient progress. This kind of closeness constructs an interactive pattern that does not allow for "a certain level of openness" (D. N. Stern, as cited in Jaffe et al., 2001, p. 145). As D. N. Stern emphasized, the high predictability associated with this close tracking can foreclose space for creativity and novelty – what Winnicott saw as so essential to emotional growth and therapeutic movement (Winnicott, 1971, p. 41). Something else is needed. *Attunement can be mutative, but its contextual meanings are pivotal to its effects.* Attention to context can give clues to when attunement can become *immaculate* and collapsing, at least in the experience of the analysand. I think this is what theories of "thirdness" (see Cooper, 2008) can help us organize if they are used "lightly" or "softly assembled" (Harris, 2005) for clinical reflection and narration. In other words, theories of "thirdness" establish a context-sensitive scope of attention for a particular interactive event that optimizes openness beyond expected categories of belief or practice which can constrict meaning-making. When this kind of constriction occurs, it is because of the way that culturally constructed categories fail to include possibilities outside of a particular scope of shared experience. The hope and promise of thirdness is to transcend such myopia whether shaped by culture or affective intensity, but usually an interaction of both.

Returning to this session, we can say that prior to this moment of shift, I am enacting, with Warren, a kind of manic defense in the rhythms of our exchange. Our rhythms construct the kind of too-close entrainment described previously, as we stay "on it" in order to stay "off it" where the "it" we are avoiding is a cataclysmic sense of fear. This manic "on-it-ness" is important to understand in the context of the unfolding development of treatment. Warren had presented some six years earlier with confusion and collapsing posture reflecting the sense of powerlessness and directionlessness that he was feeling. He described his experience of being stuck in a stagnant organization and working for a boss who was more of a tormentor than a mentor. In our early meetings, Warren described how his teenage oppositional behavior involved immersion in a drug culture and a strong need to disappoint his parents' hopes for him to be successful in some culturally "mainstream" way. He carried a kind of self-persecutory inner world into treatment where, at first, he seemed unable to find a connection to me or the process into which he was placing himself. He described how he had, at one point, early in his adult years, become active in the world of filmmaking but with little success. After some years of struggling, he became increasingly distant from his drug-using friends, a loner with little self-confidence scraping the bottom of the barrel. Somehow, some year later, Warren entered, and completed, a degree at a small community college. Later, he dragged his way into graduate school, after which he began working in this first successfully achieved, yet deadening, position at a relatively insignificant organization with no sense of inspiration or direction to offer. His early transferential experiences of me were highly idealized. From this idealization, Warren drew the motivation to apply for a much better position in a much larger and more prestigious organization. To his surprise, and quite frankly to mine also, he was hired and subsequently proceeded to blossom in his skills and accomplishments over the next few years, continually winning the "gleam in my eye" that Kohut (1966) has associated with self-object mirroring forms of recognition. Warren's triumphs over these years became a focus of coordinated "on it-ness" for both of us as I followed and accompanied his triumphant push toward culturally valorized professional status, financial reward and marriage. As such, his manic defense against trauma from the past had been simultaneously a shared construction, a pattern of high expectations for culturally "normotic" (Bollas, 1987) performance into which both Warren and I contributed.

But now, within this micro-moment, this disastrous feeling of pressured progression derailed, invades the space between us in the form of an experience of time ... time marked by absence, ... the presence of nothing, ... a pause, ... but not a "gap" or silence in the sense that a culturally Western/Northern ear normatively is entrained to organize silence, but rather a "relation" between sounds, a filling heard by the ear ... an experience for which the Greeks sitting on the border between the North and the South, reserve the term *diastema*. In the clinical moment constituted by Warren and me, the expected continuity of manic activity is disrupted by a violation, an unexpected pause in the continuum, a silence, but one that fills out a relation with powerful affective meaning, *diastema*. *Diastema* gives us a term for a different kind of metaphor for silence than space for the analysand's projection or the analyst's reverie. *Diastema* allows us to imagine silence as a co-constructed relation, not an absence of activity, but rather as an action full with significations shared.

What is this about ... this fear that fills each of our respective attentions?!?!?!?! Now the forward press of Warren's rhythm begins to vary. I can hear this in the quiver of his voice as he begins to shift his attention from all his culturally valorized triumphs and responsibilities to a narration of the sense of pain and mourning for the kind of responsiveness from both parents that was starkly missing from the timing marking his interpersonal exchanges with each of them. His previously steady, fast moving, stream is now being marked with slight accents – accents that break up the flow unexpectedly. *This rhythmic variation, in itself, communicates affective impact from him and constitutes a nascent shift in me.* I can feel it in my internal "mindlock" where I can find no thoughts and no words ... no smart clinical strategies to contain, modulate, or begin to transform Warren's emerging pain. Something in my participation is perturbed, and this faintly recognized subtle effect, first experienced in my body, quickly catalyzes a retrospective recognition of my contribution to the manic defense that we have been previously enacting in order to avoid his experiencing such a tremendous hole of emptiness and loneliness.

I have been coordinating with Warren's rapid flow in an embodied shared sense of connection, an exhilarating glide, narcissistically fulfilling a culturally reinforced sense of power and triumph. But now the shift in his rhythm catalyzes for me a different rhythmic response. I can no longer join his fast pace that, I now begin to sense, in retrospect, has created for both of us a relatively conflict-free collusion of pseudo-competence. Now my movement with Warren has suddenly become constricted by some signal within in response to something experienced in his embodied rhythms. The constriction rapidly regresses to collapse and the coordination of my responsiveness dissipates as I open a wide rhythmic chasm between his shifting accents and my responses, which are now constituting a dropping out of our flow, a violation of expectation for our previous pattern. I can no longer participate in our rhythmic coordination avoiding his pain and suffering. It is a fear and suffering with which Warrren has been both haunted in our work and from which he has carried the hope that our relating would be a form of liberation. My body can no longer collude in the rhythmic participation that avoids a way of relating that might bring about such a transformation.

The polyrhythmic weave and time as culturally constructed

Now comes that "stretched moment" for which I was trying to find description in earlier sentences – a moment that, when you are embedded in it, seems never to end. I am going to describe it and also enact it in this text as I "stretch out." "Stretch out" is a phrase from jazz jargon meaning to take a long interpretive solo, a series of variations on a particular theme or composition. The saxophonist/composer John Coltrane made famous long interpretive solos where he developed ideas into various phrasings large and small, rapidly at times, more slowly at other times, always building and expanding on the possibilities of experience that could be shaped in response to an original melody. While

Coltrane could go on for as long as an hour on one tune, I will only take a few pages here. My solo consists of a series of reflections further unfolding and contextualizing the idea of "stretched time" within a consideration of cultural differences that can shape self and other organizations of experience (and the implications for how these differences might shape clinical thinking and activity).

In the sense of time and space found in many European-based cultural expressions, there can be no such thing as a "stretched moment." Here, I am thinking of many different cultural traditions evolved over thousands of years. I am aware that in the last century or so, since the advent of audio recording, there has been a process of exchange among different cultures with particular emphasis on music, such that most music we now hear is multicultural as opposed to uni-cultural in its origins and expressions. Thus, 20th and 21st-century music throughout the planet has been increasingly influenced by traditions originating in cultural practices first taking shape below the equator, particular regarding the use of time. But I would argue that differences in complexity and sophistication are still significant. (There are also less frequently found anomalous examples of the kind of rhythmic complexity that I am emphasizing in some north-of-the-equator cultural practices emerging before the advent of recording and electronic media. Such examples can be found in Irish, Yiddish and Gypsy musical traditions of music and poetry, and I do not claim the ethnomusicological expertise to argue the origins of these practices.)

What I want to highlight is that time in most European-based traditions is linear and metric. It moves from point one to point two with measurable beats of repeating regular duration between the two points. This is the kind of metric dimension of experience that Bucci (1997) associates with symbolic representation. Such a practice creates expectations for predictable measures of contingency, affect expression, and other kinds of tension and release. Consistent with this set of cultural expectations, percussive musical instruments mark a cadenced sense of time where, to quote Lawrence Welk, the American bandleader made famous on early black-and-white television, there is "a one, 'ana' two, 'ana' three, 'ana' four". A one can never be a two. There cannot be two ones. In this Northern sense of time when there is an interval, a gap, a silence, there is an absence of something, marked by something that comes before and something that comes after the interval.

On the other hand, many cultures below the equator seem to express and experience musical time differently. Polyrhythmicity emerges out of such cultures from the African and South American continents where the ear for rhythms is socialized in a way "somewhat" similar to the way that the European/North American ear is often socialized for tonality and, as these musical traditions have developed, also harmony. The contemporary Brazilian percussionist Dende Macedo has described the polyrhythmicity of samba as drums talking with one another (personal communication, November, 2007). He explains that different styles of percussion have claves or rhythmic signatures and variations, the interaction of which make up percussive melodies. Here the tonality that one cultural practice associates with a brass, reed, or string instrument is carried by skin stretched across a hollowed-out tree or sculpted metal cylinder. Within this tonality, Dende speaks of different "songs" that one might create through the "fusion" of the different drums, each offering a particular rhythm or rhythmic variation in response to one another. For example, the internationally recognized Bahian percussive group, Olodum, is well known for their "fusion" of the reggae and samba traditions to create a variety of new rhythmic variations for song and dance. Another internationally recognized Bahian group with which Dende originally performed, Timbalada, has introduced a rhythm called levada, which creates in contrast to the uplifting, joyous combinations of reggae and samba, a light, relaxed experience. This is a rhythm in which several different kinds of drums each create a different rhythm, which in a complex combination of patterns creates the feeling of strolling down the street. And so, percussionists are heard in dialogue out of the rhythms that they create, similar to exchanges between soloists and choruses in the European choral and/or orchestral traditions.

Here is a detailed illustration of how this can work. For example, as compared to the metric function where a 1 cannot be a 2 or for that matter a 3 or a 4, when one drum is creating a pattern using a cycle of three beats and another, a pattern using a cycle of four beats, and you try to count linearly, the 1 of the first drum becomes first the 4 of the second drummer. Then, in a second cycle of exchange the 1 becomes the 3 of the second drummer. Then, in a third cycle of exchange, the 1 of the first drummer becomes the 2 of the second drummer. Then, in a fourth cycle of exchange the 1 of the first drummer becomes for a "softly assembled" micro-moment the 1 of the second drummer. Here, we have three mismatches and one match, creating a sense of novelty and positive uplifting affect. (Below is a visual representation of the relationship between the first drummer's rhythmic pattern and the second drummer's pattern. Note that the 1-beats of the first drummer are underlined and italicized and the corresponding 4-, 3-, and 2-beats of the second drummer that fall as a match with the 1-beats of the first drummer are also underlined and italicized.)

First drummer: *1* 2 3 *1* 2 3 *1* 2 3 *1* 2 3 *1* 2 3
Second drummer: *1* 2 3 *4* 1 2 *3* 4 1 *2* 3 4 *1* 2 3 4

These rhythmic dialogues constitute meanings for the participants, and for other listeners when present, evocative of deep emotional responses. Rhythm has been used to pace manual labor, galvanize dancers, rally marchers, or summon spirits by shifting accents and tempos to sooth or jolt. It is just this kind of polyrhythmicity, a kind of *psychoanalytic samba*, that I am highlighting in the subtle micro-moments of a clinical interaction by examining the exchange between Warren and me and the emergent affective meanings that are being constituted within this rhythmic dialogue. Here a form of polyrhythmicity available within a particular cultural context but not necessarily another, reveals phenomena critical for narrating analytic interaction. Polyrhythmicity thus becomes a valuable metaphor for expanding psychoanalytic discourse. Polyrhythmicity becomes a metaphor within the narration of clinical interaction, not available within the current European cultural lens which tends to valorize structure, linearity and specificity. Rather, in contrast, fluidity and nonlinear complexity is given greater significance with an Afro-Brazilian culturally derived lens. There is more that can be unpacked regarding the significance of how cultural lenses shape social constructions, both for theoretical lenses and strategies of clinical participation. I continue to develop this significance of the social in interaction with the unconscious in coming chapters.

Polyrhythmicity in the clinical interaction

How can thinking with a samba metaphor help us to clinically attend to an expanded sense of the meanings that timing can have in psychoanalytic activity? How does an ear for the *polyrhythmic weave* in the analytic encounter sharpen our sense for how linear time can be subjectively shrunk, stretched, contracted, or expanded, and thus contextualized in complex myriads of echoes and counterpoints within a clinical interaction? It is important to offer several theoretical correctives here. One most important corrective is that these temporal variations are not conceptualized as unconscious primary process events. They are recognized as intrinsic dimensions to the unfolding interactive patterning within a clinical encounter that shape significant affective meanings. Both rhythmic variation and the emerging affective meanings they can constitute can be conscious or unconscious at different points in the treatment process. In this sense the complex patterning of time and timing is intrinsic to the construction of a sense of subjective and intersubjective space. Katie Gentile (2007) provided exquisite descriptions for how different experiences of time are intrinsic to a sense of coherence, continuity and vitality in the experience of a sexually traumatized woman. Here, I am specifically using a more micro-moment lens trying to focus in on a stitch or two of the polyrhythmic weave (I prefer this metaphor to tip of the iceberg) to help us understand how the moment I just described between Warren and me becomes "stretched." But of particular clinical utility are the unconscious meanings emerging within this "stretched" experience for each of us.

Warren speaks: something about being overwhelmed with expectations from his boss. (Here his flow is still a manic forward-moving cadence, previously offered with an expectation of a matching cadence coming from me.) As Warren awaits my response, which emerges not as expected, anxiety begins to build in his face and voice. I am silent. (My pause creates a violation of the expected rhythm we have been constituting. Now a new rhythmic weave is nascent. It is a linear violation, and, at the same time, a nonlinear perturbation, the potential emergence of something with a more complex patterning than just matching.) I am thinking about Warren's need to be recognized and loved, and his descriptions of the kind of panic spin into which he can fall. He manages this fear of falling apart with nicotine, alcohol, gambling, intense sexual affairs ... anything that will fill his void of emptiness and loneliness with excitement through embodied sensations. These sensations, then, counteract a powerful surge of anesthetization constructing a sense of being out of control and terrified, into which he can recurrently fall. These manically constructed sensations paint a false self-surface-sense of coherence over a rapidly deteriorating ability to feel embodied and connected affectively to others.

My reverie, my pause (as Warren experiences it), seems to go on too long. His speech begins to fragment. (Here Warren's rhythm is shifting in response to my pause. A powerful set of affective meanings is in formation, i.e. being constituted in and between each of us.) Warren's words are still coherent. He is wondering if I am there. Am I responding? He asks, his voice tentatively attempting to form words, "Are you li ... ... li ... ... listening?" Now his voice is weak and high pitched – the sound of a scared little boy. His words begin to fragment almost into a stutter, but no, it seems to be the throat muscles that are faltering ... that seem to fail to gather the strength to construct the morphemic shapes that create the form and flow of the word sound. His voice shakes and fills with static. (Now Warren's rhythm shifts from a smooth, fast pace to a slowed-down syncopation with uneven rhythmic accents. A new patterning is emerging, the affective significance of which is becoming increasingly clear.) For me, this shift in rhythmic accent creates an impression that Warren is experiencing an escalation of fear. But, seemingly in contradiction, he also appears angry, frustrated. (There is something about Warren's accents to which

I respond, catalyzing in me multiple affective responses with multiple potential meanings.) Countertransferentially in this moment, Warren is my father disappointed ... no, infuriated that I have not met his expectation for emotional closeness that he demands ... an emotional closeness that he does not initiate or reciprocate himself. I am able to wonder, am I in the transference Warren's father or mother or both? Does my pause feel like a narcissistic fury or, possibly worse, an annihilating indifference? This "long" moment is out of control and terrifying for Warren. And for me?

My silence ... my absence of an utterance filling the space, creates a shift in the "on it" rhythms we have regularly been creating together. Where a sound is expected, no sound is experienced. But is nothing experienced? Might Warren be experiencing my silence as frustration, resentment, anger? I believe that some aspect of awareness of my participation in our interaction, not yet given conscious recognition, is a need or therapeutic imperative (coming from my professional culture or my unique voice within that cultural context) to refuse my complementary participation contributing to the drivenness of the "on it" timing in which we are entrained. My violation of the expected syncopation of our turn taking destabilizes a pattern of drivenness into which I feel we are locked together. My rhythmic accent, a pause where a rhythmic patterning driving us manically forward is expected, is more powerful in its impact than I am expecting – again, surprising me with the degree of uncertainty marking these troubled currents, the flows of which I am attempting to navigate with Warren. But my pause, a shift in timing, is also a movement that catalyzes a shift in attention as Warren's imagistic and semantic flows begin to be shaped by reconstructions of childhood, annihilations, "little murders," which our momentary but cataclysmic dysfunction is resonating into memory and utterance.

Am I out of control, terrified? Well, I am uncertain, at first, without thoughts or words to understand, contain or modulate Warren's emerging pain. But then, as the pause takes shape (a kind of slow-motion experience for me – again, a stretching of time) space opens up ... a small space ... a glimmer of light ... but enough for me to reflect that this shift in syncopation (crystallizing, in part, from my own sense of helplessness and uncertainty, an undeniable but inevitably unavoidable aspect of surrender (Ghent, 1990/1999) in these kinds of moments) is not just reconstructing an emotional crush (a rupture in rhythm). It is also constructing space, not as absence but as a tangible presence, a presence of attention that Warren might be beginning to experience in the gaze of my eyes and changing affective tension in my facial display. What I am experiencing is not just in a shift of vocal tempo but also in the shifting of muscle movements that shape Warren's gaze and facial expression signaling fear and pain. (Now a new rhythm is forming in juxtaposition with the old, a *polyrhythmic* re-patterning, creating newness.) What fills this space speaks not with words, of course, but with *new timing* that allows memories and feelings, resonating the presence and the past, in which anger and pain caused by confusion from caregivers who did not respond or support in a good-enough, rhythmically reliable enough, way, can have a place in present time and space to be named and felt. So, as Warren is shifting into this retrospective narration of his past pain, a new polyrhythmic weave is emerging between us. What fills this space, then, is a form of "language" (G. Nebbiosi, personal communication, October 13, 2007), communicating meaningful affective state and state change, a communication that is not possible to articulate in the language of words at this point. But it is a communication in rhythm that catalyzes a shift in the affective/ cognitive/kinesthetic blending that now is transforming into a new *polyrhythmicity*.

As Warren begins to talk about his pain, tears flow easily. (The short accents in his speech flow, marking his shift, now become less staccato. This flow is clearly slowed down and syncopated with unevenly spaced accents that create pause for reflection, spaces for the previously dissociated suffering to seep out and be given form and narration.) My participation at this point becomes more like a musical accompanist. In the Southern percussive tradition that I discussed earlier, there is a practice in which one drummer offers variations expressive of emergent affective experience. To support this process an accompanist (often there are two in the original religious form of this practice .... We could think of both analyst and the virtually present voice of supervision/tradition) offers a rhythm that, while different than that of the soloist creating variations, provides a counterpoint that helps to enhance the affective impact of the variations. (This is like the effects of a rhythmic cycle of 3s juxtaposed with a rhythmic cycle of 4s as in my previous illustration.)

And so, in response to Warren's shift in rhythm and narrative focus, I shift out of "mindlock" and the stretched pause which we have just micro-momentarily inhabited. Now my rhythm, different than Warren's, offers a pattern of lightly articulated beats, emerging in a non-periodic pattern, marking and/or echoing his rhythm with my accents of recognition and affirmation as he painfully recounts memories of his traumatizing encounters with his father and mother. Here, embeddedness in an enactment with Warren at first destabilizes my self-state in the clinical role of interpreter and organizer of experience shaped by my expectations for a psychoanalytic performance as a member of the larger cultural context in which I am the professional "mind healer." Here the shift in rhythm is first experienced as unexpected and disrupting the coordinated syncopation of our patterning. But then this shift also catalyzes for me an experience, breaking out of rigid culturally shaped categorization, to experience a playful interplay, fluid and multiply textured with meaning. From a moment of freeze and confusion, I begin to sense an emergent vitality that frees me from expectations shaped by the analytic and larger cultures that contextualize my self-reflections. The *polyrhythmic* weave of our accents creates a new rhythm contrasting greatly with the pressured flow in which we had begun the session. Now there is bearable movement, a dialogue of percussive melody, a psychoanalytic samba that accompanies, quietly in the background, the mourning that is being unleashed for my patient concerning his childhood suffering. Now the unspoken polyrhythms, at least for the next "stretch" of this session, constitute the kind holding (Winnicott, 1954/1975) or selfobject dimensions of transference (Kohut, 1971) that make possible a loosening of the vertical split, initiating an undoing of dissociative lockups capturing both Warren and me. These dissociations have been artfully camouflaged by our previous rhythmic patterning and the culturally structured meanings concerning power and status out of which such rhythms are constituted.

And so, it was not *nothing* that was occurring as we sat in that stretched moment of silence but, rather, a powerful mutative emotional metamorphosis emerging from a cocoon of fright and dislocation, both constituted and transformed on subtle unspoken dimensions of *polyrhythmicity*, marking old and new meanings of timing. These meanings were different for each of us and yet related by the rhythmic flows we were creating. And in this sense, even before a period of reflection on possible meanings, we began to experience new possibilities for vitality constituted by the novel syncopations of accents and pauses.

Timing, structure and fluidity

In the narration of the short stretch of time marking the heightened moment of clinical encounter between Warren and me, a panoply of affective experience unfolded for each of us. While a reader could fix on recognizable descriptions of attunement and rupture, the critical perspectival distance for what is harvested from this textual construction seems to be something different, something of a "wider ecology" (Jaffe et al., 2001). This "wider ecology" provides a lens for the analyst to "see" and "hear" a mutative patterning, a *polyrhythmic weave* in which attunement is not just an experiential moment of match; in which rupture is not just an experiential moment of mismatch. Rather, with such a lens, multiple levels of dialogic rhythm become apparent, each of which, as well as the interaction of which, constructs a wash of heterogeneous affective possibilities and meanings. To highlight this significance, let's take the opportunity that this clinical material affords to consider some other options for how the encounter between Warren and me might have unfolded, and to which I might have had conscious reflective access or not. Considering other possibilities helps to emphasize the significance of the micro-patterning of accents and pauses illustrated in this chapter.

For example, in response to Warren's comments about being overwhelmed by expectations from his supervisor, I might not have paused. Rather, I might have stayed with the "on it" rhythm formulating a verbal transference interpretation that, if effective, might have opened up a space for Warren to express feelings of being overwhelmed by expectations from me. This could have eventually moved to transferential understandings connecting Warren's experience of me to his experiences of his parents. In this case, whereas his parents seemed not to be responsive enough, my responsiveness in contrast to his expectations might have felt similar, but also, at times, to be too much, and we could explore his fears of not satisfying me, his supervisor, or others in his life such as friends and spouse. On the other hand, my verbal interpretation, however effectively structured, might have been experienced as a reenactment creating overwhelming expectations for him coming from me in ways similar to what he experienced with his boss. Were this the case, the possibility for the creation of a reflective space in this moment of treatment would have been lost.

Alternatively, as my pause became "stretched" too long for Warren, I might have noted the anxiety building in his face and then his voice. I might have attended to facial muscle shifts and shifts in tempo and tone of voice, (the fluidity rather than the structure (transference meanings) of my experience of him). This could have occurred just a bit earlier in my experience of him than occurred as I reported. This might have led to a different experience for Warren of my responsiveness than I reported. I might have broken the rhythm or feel of the pause just a fraction of a second earlier than I did by verbally inquiring about the anxiety I was observing in his face and voice. This attention might have catalyzed a new beginning experience for Warren, in which a different kind of violation than that which occurred would serve to trigger a shift in his thoughts and his sense of our interactive patterning. He may have associated to his experiences with his parents. Alternatively, my verbal inquiry might have created an experience of overwhelming expectations for him to regulate his affect, similar to his experience of expectations from his boss. In this case, rather than a new beginning for an opening for something different, Warren would have experienced my attention to nonverbal dimensions of our exchange as a reenactment of the annihilating effect of power relations he experienced at work. Again, the opportunity for a space for reflection, symbolization and verbalized association might have been lost unless we were able to notice this effect and begin to verbally reflect upon it.

In both of these formulations, while, clearly descriptions of interactions and possible emergent meanings, I am attending to and describing ways that Warren experiences me that reveal meanings frozen by a particular dynamic such as an internally experienced relational pattern of match categorized as attunement, or an internally experienced relational pattern of mismatch characterized as rupture. (These discursive categories of formulation would be the basis for my interventions.) In both of the hypothetical alternative responses coming out of different countertransferential organizations than in fact occurred, I consider how the analyst's activity could be experienced by the patient as either serving some kind of mutually regulating holding or self-object forward movement experience, or not.

The two hypothetical alternatives offer an opportunity to highlight the value of the kind of attention I am illustrating by focusing on the fluidity of polyrhythms rather than formulated meanings that might be attributed to a particular micro-moment of interaction involving Warren and me. In each alternative I understand attempts at mutual regulation with a particular discursive strategy. I use language describing internal structures representing relational dynamics. These are the conceptions that concern holding or self-object experience: two formulations that have been very helpful for understanding patterns of interactive regulation/dysregulation. But in the actual clinical encounter for which I have offered a post hoc narration, because of the dissociative process intrinsic to the enactment in which I and Warren have been caught, I have not been able to formulate any such representations for mine or my patient's internal experience. In such stretches of dissociated enactment, there are no countertransferential theoretical "life preservers" for the analyst to organize a coherent sense of activity and meaning. And from the embodied dimensions of Warren's experience that impacted me, it was not clear that he was recognizing any nurturing relational pattern. Rather, in the case for Warren (and for me), my pause became an absence, a hole filled with toxic meaning. In retrospective reflection, we can see that for that micro-moment experienced as "stretched," there seemed to be an absence of anything instructive or growth promoting in our encounter. But paradoxically, this pause, this rhythmic violation of expected patterning, also created a space for mutative symbolic reflection on the part of the analysand, a place where he was able to experience a powerful connection to affective experiences of sadness, anger and vulnerability, previously anesthetized and dissociated. I was able to formulate my awareness of this meaning, *not with attention to structural meanings, but with attention to the contours of the fluidity of the polyrhythmic weave which constituted powerful emotional impact for both Warren and me.*

What is interesting about analytic participation on registrations of fluidity is that the "information" we act upon is not available symbolically for re-presentation and reflection. In fact, such experience is rather *in-formation*, not yet fully formulated (and which may never reach a level of form), but nonetheless shaping powerful experience on non-symbolic, embodied registers of affect. For the analyst, this is a different kind of countertransference responsiveness than attunement, one that has the potential to be an alternative registration to the symbolic. (See Ingram, 2008, for consideration of signification without representation). Here is an example of *where dissociation was, embodied signification becomes.* These embodied significations then become the affective signals for meaning that might later be given verbal articulation as when I sense a shift in the rhythms Warren and I are constituting and when my rhythm then shifts to contribute to an opening of feelings in the transference that he can recognize as similar to unbearable affect, first experienced in childhood, that he previously dissociated and/or anesthetized through various forms of enactment. Embodied signification is, thus, rich and complex with clinical meanings. This kind of responsiveness, this recognition without verbalized symbolization, is what, as introduced earlier, Ghent (1990/1999) has described as surrender, but a surrender to a scope of attention constituting a "wider ecology" of fluid registrations multiply woven polyrhythmically. Surrendering to the subtle unspoken cues that this attention constitutes formed for me a focus from which I was subsequently able to narrate a sense of what Warren and I are/were doing together both consciously and unconsciously. This surrender aids my capacity to bear the vulnerability of the uncertainty of fluid experience. With this scope of attention, multiple meanings come tumbling out of the *polyrhythmicity* of our exchange. Rather than attunement, as a bidirectional moment of responsiveness, my experience of Warren and me is contextualized in a weave of interacting possibilities none of which, initially, I am able to recognize and respond to verbally. In this instance, my pause emerges (as I can report retrospectively) out of a surrender to possible significations for what is not spoken but felt on so many embodied dimensions of co-constructed rhythms, rhythms that "spoke" the ways we were affecting and affected by each other.

Chapter 3

Narrating the fluidity of micro-patterning

Found in translation perhaps

Introduction

The text of this chapter is modified from a response to discussions by Cornell (2011) and Markman (2011) concerning the original text from which the previous chapter is derived. It is included as a chapter here for the value of the careful considerations given by myself and these authors to the challenges of creating narration for experience which in itself registers not as verbal symbolic communication. I believe the discussion of how each of us sees possibilities for engaging this limitation to communication about the fluidity of micro-moment patterning of embodied rhythms is critical to a sense of the scope and limits of the mission for this or any other related exercises in written expression.

Reflections

I await the electronic arrival of the texts from Cornell and Markman ... words ... organized with grammar, syntax, signification, poetry, analysis, judgment .... Will I find myself ... feel a sense of vitalized, syncopating recognition in the phrases and rhythms of these visually packaged yet viscerally impacting pronouncements? ... or will I reel with humiliation and/or rage ... possibly collapse into a deadened space of brain freeze ... maybe a total kinesthetic anesthetization ... an unbidden micro-morph into anti-space, anti-time ... no memory, no desire, no mind, no body? My effort has been to use words to re-present, to speak, in a sense, at least, on paper (electronic screen?), tides of feelings, of emotions registering between me and my patient, Warren, in rhythmic waves of embodied sensations as not senseless or "primitive" but rather as the poetry, the ballet of signification in which we, humans, are always engaged as socially interactive subjects woven into a field of relations. I do this believing so strongly that there is potential folly, Cartesian error the Stolorow crew would have it, at least potential danger of limitation or misrepresentation, in any and every attempt to move from lived experience with all its density and endless, nonlinear possibility, to conceptualization, to representation, to constriction and memorialization within a word symbol-category and the possible word arrangements of sentences, paragraphs, etc., which are the contemporary technology of knowledge valorized in post-Gutenberg cultural space – a space we inhabit as this text is produced and consumed. But this other form of knowledge, maybe even a kind of wisdom, this embodied yet unable to be spoken (or really written) ... I, Cornell (2011), Markman (2011), and others too (I am thinking of all the authors in Anderson, 1998, 2008, as well as recent voices that have pursued a similar effort to mine (Gentile, 2007; La Bare, 2005; Shapiro, 1996, 2009; Sonntag, 2006, to name a few)), seem to agree is worth *trying* to write about. Trying to write about is not the same as capturing in words. Capturing ... to put a cap on, as if some kind of toxic spill needing to be capped ... this kind of writing delineates, yes, but constricts ... a point, a moment, a structure, a frame frozen in time where geometric arrangements can be described for their potential dynamic significance. *This kind of writing fails to evoke movement.* We write ... using the term "working through" (Markman extending Freud's chess metaphor calls it the "middle game ... left to silence, and perhaps intuition" (2011, p. 437)) .... But how? ... In what way? ... with what spectrum and cadence of state and state shifts for analyst and for patient and with what interactive metamorphic significance ... the kind of tipping points (see Chapter 4) ... the enactments, the rupture, the breakdowns and breakthroughs ... the stuff unfolding in time, yes not timing (as with Glover, 1931/1955), but motion, rhythms cascading against and through ... the waves of emotion, polyrhythmically, at times rushing, at times trickling, at time flowing unnoticed toward forms of recognition? ... communion? ... "mutative moments"???

Can we write in some way, not to capture and re-present *structure* … but to invoke a sense of movement, of fluidity, complex, slippery, chaotic in the sense of unpredictably shifting, yet elegant in its choreography as it reveals patterning in time … time not just as a linear event which the unconscious can collapse, twist or shuffle, but timing as multiply syncopating pulses of movement continually interacting and shifting, spinning out, spinning off or into structure, sometimes softly assembled, sometimes scaffolded for long stretches of life unfolding … rhythms breathing life and passion? This is a "widened ecology" (Jaffe, Beebe, Feldstein et al., 2001), a different way of encountering experience central to contemporary psychoanalytic understanding and activity. This is an approach and an ecology in recognition of the complex difficulties involved in being found and/or translated as a patient, analyst or theorist.

Given the aforementioned concern, Cornell and Markman both read my work with Warren in a way that I have felt *found* (there is much agreement across our three texts) … but also translated. Translation, according to my computer dictionary, is something like an algorithm, a form of conversion. Cornell (2011) has suggested we can read Winnicott (1949/1958a) in a way that converts a way of reading Freud and Reich into something beyond the effects of either.

> Winnicott's transformation of the Freudian and Reichian premises is in his recognition of the necessity of an other's repeated attention to and languaging of somatic experience that situates the mind in the body, the psyche–soma as the foundation for a robust sense of self in the world.
>
> Language can be in the service of the body rather than in place of or competition with it, facilitating an ease of flowing self-contact between the unlanguaged subsymbolic orders with those of the verbal symbolic realms that have been so long the primary domain of the analytic endeavor.
>
> (Cornell, 2011, p. 434)

Cornell offers this conceptual renovation as a way to think about the events I narrate in my work with Warren, to which he adds possible linguistic texture where I did/could not.

Something is happening here. I went quiet inside, like my words disappeared. Slowing down. You, too? There's a shift in the way you are speaking. Can you hear the tone in your voice? Something has changed between us ..... (pausing) A kind of disturbance. And a kind of slowing down. An opening up. My breathing has changed ... Your face. Notice what's happening in your body .... Take your time. Just notice.

The analyst's words are descriptive, slowly paced, exploring, wondering, inviting. The therapeutic invitation is for a kind of somatic attending, a sort of body-level free association, perhaps brought into words, perhaps not, but facilitated by both the analyst's words and the way of speaking those words. The analyst offers attention, recognition, rather than interpretation—a minding of the body.

(Cornell, 2011, pp. 433–434)

Cornell, in a sense, converts my narrative, my activity, into another possibility. He calls this "somatic attending" where attention becomes a form of regulation (interactive, at least, if not both self and interactive) or what I am now describing as *navigation*, rather than interpretation. Here attention is understood for its action within the fluidity of interaction rather than simply as a move to structure, define, interpret. "Somatic attending" begins to re-present in body-based description, the movement, the states and state shifts, embodied and not yet re-presented. Such attention is in the service of ordering, but not just as an act of structuring through interpretation.

Markman (2011), on the other hand, calls on us to be wary of providing attention that might bring order. His central effort to distinguish my approach from his comes with his use of the term *dissonance* to delineate an important aspect of experience that my term *polyrhythmic weave* seems to miss. Markman wants to hear more about the analyst's intentionality – my intentionality with my patient, Warren. He emphasizes the clinical importance of the analyst's intentionality in the creation of the kind of "diastema" that occurred between Warren and me. Converting Schoenberg's musical recognition of the "liberation of dissonance" to psychoanalytic purposes Markman (2011) offers this:

If 'weave' suggests a kind of binding and togetherness, the musical metaphor I suggest looks to ways that dissonance is liberated; how analysis offers an opportunity to leave the safe confines of a 'tonal center' (habit, familiarity, what is already known) and move into tonal realms uncomfortable for both analyst and patient. The metaphor of dissonance attempts to grasp what in the present moment cannot be tolerated, for reasons of anxiety in both participants, and thus cannot be symbolized.

(2011, p. 438)

For Markman *weave* invokes something coming into. He wants to emphasize, with *dissonance*, the conditions for this coming into that have to do with something coming, or that has come, apart. To contextualize his conception within the psychoanalytic cannon and beyond, Markman notes terms that have been used to express the idea of how to create the conditions for dissonance. These include Bion's idea of "detachment" as different than indifference, or Bion's idea of "caesura," a term adapted from poetry; Green's concept of the "creative negative" and "negative space" adapted from painting and similar to Miles Davis's well-known use of space in jazz improvisation; and again, from poetry, Keats's term "negative capability." In a footnote, he quotes Keats: "I mean Negative Capability, that is when men [*sic*] is capable of being in uncertainties, mysteries, doubts without any irritable reaching after facts and reason" (Markman, 2011, p. 442).

This quote from Keats becomes important to sorting out the degree of fit or difference between how Markman and I think about my clinical narrative with our respective terms (words). While acknowledging that I may be using terms different than those he favors from his Bionion/Kleinian background, he believes with the metaphor *polyrhythmic weave* that I fail to capture an important aspect of what is occurring emotionally, which he would describe as *projective identification*. Here we are in a space for conversion of words/terms and how they do or do not translate across cultures. In this case we are looking across different theoretical cultures But the problem arises over and over again across social differences shaped by political and economic arrangements as addressed in Chapter 6. This challenge/problem is further complicated when such words/terms emerge or not, in various cultural/social contexts. Markman writes:

> Knoblauch had the intention to disrupt. How had he come to this? This important question is left unanswered [Markman, 2011, p. 443]. I am inclined to reach for metaphors that allow as much for disentanglement and frayed edges, as weave [p. 444]. This experience of pressure—so central to the interaction—might be brought into the metaphor. I am wondering, after being plunged into this intense emotional matrix, why the language becomes so disembodied and abstract at this point. I understand that Knoblauch draws on a literature I do not master, but the effect for me, anyway, is to become distanced rather than connected by the language that gathers around the metaphor [p. 441].
>
> (Markman, 2011)

Markman has zeroed in on a critical aspect confronting, and I would suggest confounding, in its pressure on us as analysts to manage the impact of the polyrhythmic "waves" of emotional disruption, including fragmentation, distancing, and dissociation that can (and did) occur in a clinical episode like the one I describe with Warren. To highlight the dilemma (or challenge) Markman frames, I use his own words and their significance:

> We learn from these humbling moments, as we recognize our endless capacity to be unaware how we are participating, to be other than in our idealized (from one's own theoretical perspective) role. That is, we recognize that we are decentered, not at a particular moment, but in every moment.
>
> [...] Contrary to Kleinian and Bionian notions of projective identification, which involve state of mind—phantasies—Knoblauch's metaphor brings out with great sensitivity the relation of two bodies together.
>
> (Markman, 2011, pp. 339–440)

Given Markman's recognition of humility evoked by the limits of an analyst's awareness in moments such as the one I have described in my work with Warren (a humility required, I would suggest, to manage our capacity to "be other than in our idealized ... role"), we are aided in our efforts when we recognize, as Markman does, that we have lost control of our state(s) of mind as we have become "with great sensitivity" absorbed (Phillips, 1997, p. 744, 1999, p. 86) in a "relation between two bodies together." As Markman observes, "Rather than a lexical record of the conversation, we are paying attention to atmosphere, texture, and mutual affective influence in the interaction" (p. 437).

For me, a lexical record of the conversation is a way of capturing a description of linear projective and counterprojective representational structures that emerge from the polyrhythmic textures of the interaction. I earlier used a metaphor of a tennis ball being hit back and forth (Knoblauch, 1997) for this kind of exchange. But we are here really dealing with at least two, if not more, tennis balls in motion, with the tennis balls representing multiple states in motion – a kind of motion that becomes too dense and uncertain to navigate with intent. The recording or capturing represented with the term *projective identification* is too linear and one-dimensional. This term does not account for the very valuable and important registrations of affective state and state change carried on various embodied registrations. These state changes are too subtle or dense to become consciously aware of, as they are occurring within the complex patterning of interaction on these levels of exchange. To be intentional requires a capacity to reflect and represent that is not yet present for me in the uncertainty and density of the encounter I describe with Warren. Such a capacity to reflect is, though, subsequently precipitated by the wave of embodied experiences which initially impact my awareness.

And so, while Markman is wondering where my intentionality comes from and emphasizes the importance of intentionality for a model that is built on the therapeutic value of disruptions such as the one I describe, I would ask whether the question of intentionality is the significant question regarding this issue. Rather, my intent is, as

Markman recognizes, not to create a model but an approach. This approach is one of navigating an unpredictable process in contrast to translating experience through the lens of theory. By expanding attention to often subtly registered signals, enacted communications in the analytic exchange, the analyst sustains a struggle shaped by disequilibrating experience and loss of cognitive organizational capacity. Such struggle precipitates intuitive bridges shaped by muscular tensions, facial configurations, pauses and punctuations in speech flow, or embodied movements cross-modally choreographed.

For me, here as in other illustrations in this text, the key term is *navigational strategy* rather than intentionality. I believe that this term emerges from the significance of Ghent's (1999) formulation of the term *surrender* as an active stance of approach most facilitative for fostering the kind of analytic attention similar to Keats's notion/approach, "negative capability," that is, the capacity for "being in uncertainties, Mysteries, doubts without any irritable reaching after fact & reason." For me, intentionality implies a capacity for the analyst to re-present in some way for reflection and possible therapeutic action, a pattern of lived experience. It is the creation of a third position/perspective (Benjamin, 2009), (a theoretical life preserver if you will ... helpful, of course ... if possible), transforming or transcending the trap of projective identification, a capacity that might emerge for the analyst *at a micropoint, after, but not during, the kind of* "being in uncertainties, mysteries, doubts without any irritable reaching for fact & reason" that a stance of surrender with such a "navigational strategy" might allow. This *surrender* and *navigation*, an attempt to evolve with my word/terms, however abstract, what it feels like to give attention to the embodied but not re-presented, is subtly but significantly different than *intentionality*. It consists of the kind of humility that is involved with the different descriptions of *witnessing* offered by Gerson (2009), Grand (2000), Orange (1995), and Reis (2009). (See a further discussion of witnessing as embodied communication in Chapter 5.) This stance aims more for Phillips's idea of absorption than understanding, in a way, shifting the meaning of understanding to "something more" (Boston Change Process Study Group, 2005) or different, than symbolic definition … to a kind of intuitive embodied participation, powerful with emotional signification.

Having distinguished Markman's emphasis on intentionality from my emphasis on navigation, I want to move toward agreement with Markman recognizing that my navigational surrender is described in my narrative of Warren and myself as catalyzing an opening for intentionality and verbal symbolic representation for patient and, subsequently, analyst. This does not/cannot always occur. But there it did. Clearly, in my "approach" I *intend to be able to surrender* (though I don't claim to be able to know beforehand if and when that surrender might be evoked within the clinical interaction). And I *intend to attend* to our embodied experiences. This intentionality is based on a kind of Bionion faith (Bion, 1977, pp. 31–33), a faith in the significatory potential of a *trajectory of uncertainty* (Gentile, 2007, p. 28) to provide patterning as a basis for meaning creation. Here, while no less abstract than any of the terms used by Markman or me, terms contributed by Cornell help to elaborate this "approach."

Cornell (2011) invokes Quinodoz's (2003) term, "incarnate language" as a "'*language that touches* as one that does not confine itself to imparting thoughts, verbally, but also conveys feeling, and the sensations that accompany those feelings' (p. 35)" (Cornell, 2011, p. 433). In his words, Cornell is advocating a "language that is experience-near, language that conveys a felt sense of one's interior and somatic states. Incarnate language is a kind of speaking *to* the analysand's body rather than speaking *about it*" (p. 433). Cornell explains that he emphasizes the "communicative intentions of bodily activity, utilizing the notion of interrupted gestures" (p. 433). His term "interrupted gestures" sounds to me similar to Markman's term "dissonance." Here the importance of disruption is seen as critical. My question is whether disruption needs to be intentional. I experience such disruptions described with Warren as implicitly inevitable, unavoidable and of particular value in their unbidden arrival.

I have always assumed that the term *resonance* may be too antiseptic in its common usage in psychoanalysis. As we are now beginning to better understand the pleasures and terrors of absorption in relating that can constitute the conditions for the emergence of significant meanings, resonance is better conceptualized as more than just an experience of matching – being matched/meeting/connecting. It is a far more complex and nonlinear encounter of interacting with otherness forged within a *polyrhythmic weave* that rescues and/or sustains vitality and movement. This kind of definition for resonance includes the dissonance that according to Markman can carry emergent meaning. I discuss this kind of phenomenon in my 2000 text (Knoblauch, 2000, pp. 131–148). This phenomenon seems to be what Seligman points to in his discussion of the tipping point (see Seligman, 2005). This kind of tipping point can pop up and just as quickly dissolve, moving through moments of order, disorder and/or reordering. This process is a simultaneous psychic and interactive reorganization. It registers first as embodied, in the service of movement and vitality, and – at least for a micro-moment – as a softly assembled state of self and/or interactive regulation (Beebe, Knoblauch et al., 2005; Harris, 2005). See Saketopoulou, 2019, for a different vision emerging from an innovative reading spanning Freud, Laplanche, Stein, Dimen and others, which queries the valorizing of regulation and illustrates the mutative significance of affective dysregulation, particularly an emotional too-muchness to which she gives the term *overwhelm*.

Within this expanded conceptualization of weave, as Cornell (2011) observes, language, can be in the service of the body rather than in place of or in competition with it, facilitating an ease of flowing self-contact between the unlanguaged sub-symbolic orders with those of the verbal, symbolic realms that have been so long the primary domain of the analytic endeavor (p. 434).

I hold Cornell's optimism for language in the service of the body in tension with mine and Saketopoulou's recognition of the significance for the dysregulating, transgressive and subversive breakthroughs of the unspeakable haunting that we and our patients inevitably/unavoidably conjure in our attempts at encounter as embodied subjects. I have tried to illustrate the value of bearing up emotionally within the tension of the particular form of weave or interaction between the unlanguaged and the verbal in Chapters

1 and 2. I pursue this project in other ways later in this text. Clearly the effort to translate the unlanguaged for clinical strategy, though enhanced by the exchange between Cornell, Markman and myself, continues. We have each offered worded attempts to invoke a sense, with narrative and analysis, of the processes by which weavings of coming apart and coming into (Saketopoulou, 2019 uses the terms binding/unbinding) create patterning on embodied registers as meaning in formation. These attempts at description contribute to the possible therapeutic advantages of the attentional "approach" I illustrate in Chapters 1 and 2. Perhaps the term *polyrhythmic weave* might serve as a metaphor invoking the tearing apart prerequisite to, and, as well as, coming together, the dissonance within the resonance, or as Winnicott has helped us to harness in our psychoanalytic understanding: the place of destruction of form(s) in the process of creating something new. Should we now not think/speak/write so much of formulated versus unformulated, but more about the *trans*-formed? Perhaps there is a better metaphor for these processes, given the historical use of the term "resonance" in our field. Perhaps the kind of absorption we are reaching for, which includes the dissonance and marking about which Markman and Cornell write, might be better invoked with a word suggesting the participatory uncertainty of encounter with resonant/dissonant experience. Perhaps Saketopoulou's recent synthesis of a Freudian and Laplanchian lens (as refracted through queer theory and the vernaculars developed in *subcultural* communities) to name experiences such as *overwhelm, sexual* and *limit consent* can guide and support the analytic project in a different more helpful way. Perhaps …

Chapter 4

Between body, culture and subjectivity

The tensions of passion and custom

Encountering Frannie and her dream

In a Friday session, Frannie describes her experience sitting in church feeling a deep sense of confirmation that she should choose a road of adventure, pursuing an opportunity to do important work in a country other than the USA; somewhere she has developed relationships with church personnel and health care providers who have benefited,, and would continue to benefit, from her presence and contributions to their work, bringing needed services to the community there. This decision comes within the context of her having a lover abroad and the painful conflict she experiences over her ambivalence about divorcing her husband. That decision is occurring within a cultural history constituted as part of a religious Catholic family where pleasure and wrongness are too frequently conflated and which conflation totally obscures questions of agency and vitality. What kind of response does Frannie expect this statement will trigger from her analyst and with what significance to her own subjectivity? What does this decision have to do with her marital difficulties and how she experiences my responses to these? How might my personal history and marital status be affecting her or my subjective experience of this moment? How might each of these considerations be related to Frannie's experience of the impact of her passion and the different cultures through which she has been commuting?

Frannie describes how, sitting in church, she is almost visited with a sense of confirmation, a sense that there is a right and a wrong surrender for her. As indicated in some of her significant dreams, Frannie and I have arrived at this point of awareness in previous sessions. Frannie's dreams reflect a relentless conflict between staying and going. As an example, in one recent dream, her childhood friends are driving her to the airport to catch a plane to join her lover but they continually frustrate her as they miss turns that lead to the airport ... (an imaginative configuration of different self-states reflecting her internal confusion and ambivalence in sorting out her decision). She worries that she would miss her plane and lose the opportunity to be with her beloved. The dreams begin to reveal more about her subjective sense of herself and her relationship to otherness. In another dream, she is having pleasurable sex with her husband, who asks her why she is having sex with him if she is going to leave him (a decision that she has not consciously made at the time of the dream). The scene then shifts to being in a car her husband is driving. Frannie is in the back seat having sex with herself. She is surprised to find she has a penis. In her associating to the dream, she speaks about the power she feels over her husband. She feels she must be the one who sets the direction and initiates action in all realms of their shared activity including sex.

In a more recent dream, she describes a disturbing scene consisting of two of her best female friends from abroad killing a dog. She watches from car window as she passes by. In her associating to this scene, she reflects that though she could imagine that Americans would view this event as barbaric, in her dream she understands and accepts the killing as a necessary and reasonable practice within the culture in which it occurs. She is still in the car, not part of this culture whose normative practices and beliefs make sense to her, maybe even more sense than those that have shaped her life as an American thus far. She explains how in the dream she is feeling that the behavior of her good friends is not cruel but compassionate. She then associates to a recent encounter with her husband in which she has now told him that she will begin to arrange to leave him and end their marriage as she feels, under the circumstances of her unresolvable dilemma, that this is the most compassionate direction to take. I wonder out loud whether Frannie believes I feel that leaving her husband is barbaric.

I wonder if the car might be a safe space within which she can reflect on events from a distance, as in our treatment space, but still not feel connected to them as she in fact wants to feel. Could she still be having with me the experience of being constricted by my anticipated judgments of her as she struggles to find her own authenticity and agency? Her response is that these speculations seem right but she finds no release from her conflict coming from my verbalizing these possibilities.

Here I begin to gain a sense of how Frannie's cross-cultural experience is impacting the conflicts with which she struggles in her experience of her marriage and the monocultural traditions of family and religion in which she has been held in such a tight grip. Here, I also begin to reflect on the differences and similarities between my cultural history and hers. I wonder in reverie in what ways Frannie's sense of me as a Euro-American and married (which she has previously indicated she believes because of a reference I make to the difficulties of sustaining an intimate tie) might color our interaction and her ongoing conflict. I will return to these considerations in the coming pages.

As the last dream fragment and association suggests, Frannie feels she is moving closer to a resolution of her dilemma, at least in how it concerns her marriage. But even with an apparent decision about her external affairs, her internal conflict persists. Frannie is a 30-something daughter of first-generation, Italian American, practicing Catholics. Her grandparents, whom she loved and idealized, imbued her with a strong sense of the importance of family cohesiveness and the importance of carrying forward "traditional" values. (This was an American lower middle-class socio-economic space marked by a shared norm of distrust of change and otherness). Frannie was a "good" Italian/Catholic girl. But she had secrets and feared the judgments of others lest they discover the ways in which she violated the teachings of Catholicism. In her early adulthood, Frannie had delightedly discovered that a good childhood friend from whom she kept many secrets, particularly about her sexual experiences in adolescence, had, in fact, been doing the same with her. Their sharing tales of norm violation gave each a sense of power.

Frannie believes that she can't know for certain how much of her leaving for work and a new partner abroad might be a repeat of her childhood secret "bad girl" violations of the family and church norms that provided security and a sense of reliability and stability to her life. At the same time, she continues to experience those practices and beliefs, rooted in the past, as annihilating her capacity to creatively generate an expanding expression of her skills and passions as well as a deepening of the quality and range of her relational capacities. To surrender to the norms of her family, community and church seems to be a malevolent version of surrender, a masochistic submission (Ghent, 1999). To surrender to the adventure, challenge and passion of new professional opportunities and a different kind of partner – better educated and with a wider range of interests and activities – seems to be a different kind of surrender: an act of freedom, expressing mastery at navigating and negotiating internal conflict. (This is occurring within her present socio-economic space in which cross-cultural awareness is valued and characterized by norms of strong faith in constructive change, recognition of, and respect for, otherness, particularly as it might be characterized by different customs.)

Despite the rational analysis we can bring to these options, giving a value of malevolence to one and benevolence to another form of surrender, Frannie finds herself a vacillating captive to a continuous sense of being overwhelmed by an unresolvable dilemma. She is powerfully drawn to each option with a foreboding sense of uncertainty and fear that she will do the *wrong* thing. Reflection and analysis of her struggles come quite easily to this articulate and well-educated professional, in sharp contrast to the collapse of options and internalized persecutory voices of family, community and religion – voices that continue to capture her in stasis.

Sitting in the chair opposite me, her posture is typically relaxed as she positions her hips facing toward me in my chair. Usually, I sit with a matching posture. My hips are similarly positioned so that my body faces hers. Our postures seem in a configuration of "good enough" mutual mirroring, creating a sense of secure connection. In these moments, Frannie's gaze is intensely on my face. This, again, is also typical of her presentation. She often seems to search my face for clues that I am understanding her experience, or that I may have some unanticipated response that could represent a new and additional understanding. It is important to add that my impression of these kinds of gaze meetings has been that Frannie's intense scanning of my face often feels like the kind of hypervigilance characteristic of a child who is expecting either a transgressive response or non-responsiveness from the other.

Frannie's voice in subsequent moments becomes slightly, but noticeably, higher pitched than at other times. I have come to recognize this register in pitch as often accompanying/signaling the self-doubt in which she becomes totally absorbed as the dilemma of her ambivalence becomes unbearable. In these moments, I am often feeling an ego-dystonic sense of being a particular kind of other in the transference, a ghost projection haunting Frannie's sense of her own "truths." In reverie I wonder,

> Am I a priest/nun from her childhood experience handing out punitive judgments about violations of a strict code of conduct for living, and which Frannie might experience as blocking any expression of her own creativity or vitality? Or could I be the grandparents or father, carrying such a set of religious beliefs for 'acceptable' social conduct, constantly surveying the activities and choices of his granddaughter/daughter, lest she stray into a damned way of life?

Choosing to work in a different country entails not just leaving her marriage. Does it mean she will terminate treatment? Does Frannie feel damned by me for choosing to leave treatment? Am I damned angry at her for making such a choice? And what might be the basis for such a powerful affective response? Here I begin to experience the clash of different cultural norms, not only in Frannie's experience, but also in mine, as I grapple with my internalized expectations for clinical performance coming from my subjective sense of the psychoanalytic culture in which I am embedded, in contrast to my personal reactions to my struggling, courageous patient. Here my emotional experience suggests different meanings than my cultural context might privilege.

For Frannie to join her lover/fiancé abroad could be a dangerous and destructive enactment of the ways in which she secretly lived an alter life, a "delinquent" response to the family and religious beliefs of her childhood culture. Was this secret life of violation a false or true self-expression (Winnicott, 1960, pp. 148–150)? On the other hand, could choosing a new life abroad also represent generativity/creativity leading to an expansion of forms of self-expression and relatedness, previously constricted, if not annihilated, by an inner object world constructed out of early relationships of nonrecognition and fear-driven narcissistic psychic colonizations by parents and other authority figures, particularly driven by religious beliefs?

Entering the dense complexity of micro-moment body registrations

In moments similar to this one in which Frannie becomes paralyzed by her ambivalence, I have noted around Frannie's eyes and forehead a tightening of muscles and creasing of skin, signaling tension beneath. In these instances, Frannie seems uncertain what to expect from this other ... me. Will I confirm or correct her? Or will I respond in a way that sustains an openness to both or additional options? This kind of response of openness to change and difference, which can seem analytically focused and therapeutically appropriate in many instances, can be (and I have come to recognize, has often been) experienced by Frannie as an annihilation of the meaning of the newness and sense of agency to what she has offered. It's as if not to raise some kind of critical inquiry (which could be a willingness to be open to change, but also, and this is the challenge), could be a veil for disapproval, an inauthentic avoidance, a glossing over of the significance for her and possibly others, including myself, of this struggle. "You've got to be enraged at me for leaving you!" I sense my discomfort with being scanned and possibly experienced in these ways. In part, I feel as if I am being constructed as a violator of her voice and agency. With equal significance, I am reminded of my own experiences growing up in a working-class cultural milieu where I developed a similar kind of expectation for punitive judgment from authority figures. Here, a clash for me is between my concordant identification with Frannie and internalized norms constructing a particular set of expectations for how I should understand and respond to transference meanings shaped by the professional community with which I identify. I am wondering how these reflections are shaping the unfolding of our interactions and each of our experiences of self and other. I am struggling with my desire to continue a good treatment with a bright, self-reflective patient, and a voice within me that vicariously identifies with the risk-taking, open person following her passion, firmly seated in the center of the power of her convictions to leave her husband, her country, and me.

But *here in this micro-instant* as Frannie represents in words her move from ambivalence to decisiveness, *Frannie's body and the meaning it seems to convey have shifted.* She is leaning forward in her chair as if perched for action, maybe even confrontation. I don't feel that she is unrelaxed, but feel her alert readiness while still relaxed in a different way than previously, now communicates to me a vitality compared to a sense of resignation, even avoidance, that it has often seemed to carry previous to this moment. There is a different muscular configuration to her facial display. It impacts me as a wave of shifting emotions. She seems to be smiling *but it is a sly smile, as if to suggest she has found something somewhere within or without or both, that I won't be able to undo ... even unintentionally.* Here, her power to stand up to my power is palpable. The pitch of her voice, as she announces the outcome of her church reflections is not in that range I described earlier, but rather slightly lower, enough to signal a kind of strength, different from what I usually encounter.

But it is not just the changes in the embodied dimensions of her self-presentation that are different and seem significant. These are, of course, intrinsic to the moment as I sense a shift in the tension in the air. The tension is not just an internal dilemma between right and wrong at this point. At least, such a dilemma is not in the foreground of experience for me, and I perceive Frannie to be similarly focused. Rather, the tension in the room is potentially a "crunch" that could occur between the two of us as I might be experienced transferentially as the grandparent/father, consciously or unconsciously carrying expectations and beliefs in custom and practice, a cultural net of habits constituted to "crush" her creative but "transgressive" thought and actions in the "crunch" between her passions and previously internalized values concerning custom. Although intra-psychic conflict can be identified objectively at this point, the distinction between internal and external collapses for both of us, subjectively, at this moment of crunch between passion and culture. It is not as if culture is internalized in a mind, or inscribed on a body. Butler writes,

> Categories of true sex, discrete gender and specific sexuality have constituted the stable point of reference for a great deal of feminist theory and politics ... But is there a political shape to women,' as it were, that precedes and prefigures ... their interests ...? How is that identity shaped, and is it a political shaping that takes the very morphology and boundary of the sexed body as the ground, surface, or site of cultural inscription?
>
> (Butler, 1990, pp. 128–129)

It is as a blur where experiences of passion and culture cannot be subjectively or intersubjectively differentiated. Is Frannie, or am I, an agent of self-direction or caught unconsciously in a web of cultural imperatives constructed for how to think, feel or act?

In this moment, I am quickly becoming aware of the shift that Frannie's embodied state is catalyzing in me. I am excited about this change. My excitement is, in part, the narcissistic pleasure I am taking in the recognition that I am achieving some awareness of what her body seems to be conveying, consistent with and central to the kind of vision I and others previously offered for the mutative potential of this kind of expanded therapeutic attention on the part of the analyst (Knoblauch, 2000, 2005 – for additional discussion of the significance of attention to this implicit embodied level of dyadic exchange, see also Alfano, 2005; Anderson, 1998; Aron, 1998; Beebe et al., 2005; Dimen, 1998; Gentile, 2007;

Gunsberg & Tylim, 1998; Harris, 1998; Jacobs, 1986, 1991, 1994; Kimble Wrye, 1996, 1998; La Barre, 2001, 2005; Lyons-Ruth, 1999; McLauglin, 2005; Orbach, 1999, 2003, 2004, 2006; Shapiro, 1996; Sonntag, 2006; Sletvold, 2014; Stern, 2004). But my excitement is also precipitated by a keen sense of, at least, some of my own embodied experience that is specific to how Frannie is impacting me at this critical point. This is an embodied nonsymbolic level of countertransference experience, which I can attempt post hoc (given the limitations noted in the previous chapter), to transduce into the symbolization of word meanings in this written narrative.

I would describe these non-symbolized dimensions of my experience in the following way. My level of internal activation has been increased and I am sitting up a bit straighter and more ready to be receptive and responsive than has been my tendency. This is information for Frannie, in addition to whatever semantic meaning I might communicate with my words or not. To be more specific, as I am beginning to become aware of the shift, I realize that I have previously often matched her relaxed posture and that this matching can send, and may have been sending, a signal of collusion with her states of resignation and frustration with her stasis. (In other words, my embodied rhythm joined, in resignation and collapse, with her embodied rhythm, through my unconscious matching of posture and the potential meanings that embodied mutuality might have for each of our subjectivities.) My signal of collusion could be based on my own, until now, unreflected-upon narcissistic bias toward marriage to which I have made a commitment. On the other hand, could I be unconsciously cheering for my patient to escape the psychic confinement of the constricting cultural norms that grip her and which I have experienced in my own early history?

So, now in this moment, I can feel how my eyes are open wider than usual. My eyebrows are raised. I am wondering if my face is not expressing a sense of recognition and even, maybe, surprise. I am about to speak. This could be critical to whether my surprise is experienced in the realm of shock and judgment, however subtle, that might trigger for Frannie an internal slide into a sense of being *wrong*. How to respond? Here I am haunted, similarly to my patient, by the fear of doing the *wrong* thing, a powerful illustration of intersubjective resonance on an unsymbolized dimension of exchange that can carry the same affective impact as a symbolized verbalization. Here to be *wrong* is to constitute an enactment co-constructed on subtle unspoken but embodied dimensions of experience, in which we are both defeated by our non-conscious acceptance of a culturally contextualized normative binary that, in fact, neither of us consciously believes. My countertransference dilemma is given further denseness by the confusion between being *wrong* within a set of expectations for conduct shaped by religious and socio-economic codes, and expectations coming from a set of professional codes of conduct. Here, for me, there is an intersection of potentially toxic binaries constituted by the multicultural dimensions of the contexts that grip my interaction with Frannie.

What happens next is not something that I was able to shape out of my reverie or any predetermining therapeutic guidelines. It is something I am increasingly coming to recognize, always post hoc, as a central aspect of the kind of shift or *tipping point* that this moment I am describing becomes. (See Thelen, 2005; Piers, 2005; Seligman, 2005 for a discussion of the utility of the tipping point concept coming from nonlinear dynamic systems theory for psychoanalytic activity.) Such clinical moments are characterized by subtle somatic or kinesthetic shifts (see Cornell, 2011, 2015 as discussed in the previous chapter) occurring at a *micro-process* level of analysis compared to the more usually attended-to *structural* level of analysis. (This distinction is given further development in the next chapter.)

And so, as Frannie describes her decision to leave her husband, arrived at in deep reverie occurring in a most powerful architecturally symbolic context (a church) for the practices, rituals and traditions against which her decision will fly, I shift my body in relation to a perceptible shift in her body and tone of voice. I am sensing something that I now narrate to you with the following words which I emphasize were not in thought form in the moment I attempt to describe here. This is the symbolic description of what my body experience seemed to be speaking to me without words:

I am impacted by the decisiveness of Frannie's decision ... that she is not seeming to look for my reaction to her thoughts as she usually does, but rather I feel her delivering an announcement with firmness and resolve for which discussion has passed. This feels different. She looks and sounds different and I am responding differently to my experience of the clarity and resolve in her eyes, her body, and the tone and meaning of her words.

I do not speak of the rhythm (in part vocal and in part embodied movement) of our exchange. I can't in the moment. I am still caught up in constituting it with my response. But in this narrative, I want to focus my analytic lens upon this brief moment of exchange to observe (post hoc) and describe the shape and feel of this moment in order to illustrate how it was different from a pattern that had previously become entrained between us and how the shift of this rhythm tipped the previous state of tensions between Frannie's passion and the social customs that contextualized her judgments and emotions. This moment, a tipping point, marked the beginning of a new kind of entrained rhythm in her interactive experience with me and others.

Now, let me slow down and rewind (so to speak) the previous moment Frannie and I constituted. Frannie's shift forward in her chair, accompanied by her sly smile and lower (and I now add slower) vocal utterances, felt (in retrospect) paradoxically as if she had subtly applied a brake to shift something in our pacing and cadence. I say paradoxically because there was not so much a slowing down as a shifting, with both slowing in speech flow but a kind of acceleration or expansion in expressed vitality, a sense of growing strength in tone (lowered), pace (slowed) and body (presenting directly with poise compared to the reduced tonus in muscular effort and a sense of withdrawal in posture that was so familiar in the recent and typical rhythms of our exchange). These multimodal, non-symbolized body dimensions of Frannie's presentation, at the same time accompanied by a semantic dimension of her speech, the symbolic meaning of which was of equal significance, catalyzed a significant shift in my rhythmic accompaniment to her shift. This shift occurred on registrations of posture and activation. My posture and activation shifted to meet hers. I cannot say how my face or gaze might have been experienced by Frannie. But I can say that within the brief micro-second of our shift from resignation and defeat, to vitalized triumph and liberation, as carried in the rhythms of our body dialogue, I sensed, in the slyness of Frannie's smile, a feeling and meaning of triumphant reversal of a power gradient. This power gradient had been constituted within the repeated psychic annihilations for her in past experiences of *crunch* between passion and custom, a *crunch* and its reversal, which I am here attempting to trace in her experience of and with me as well as in her past.

What does this body shifting in the consulting room have to do with subjectivity, and even more, the nexus of the bidirectional impact of Frannie's passion and culture?

Frannie could have experienced me transferentially as critical and dismissive of her announcement to violate the codes of the tradition that had held her so tightly in earlier years, and still in her present psychic states. But (despite my concern for being *wrong* in the terms of, at least, two different cultural codes for practice and belief) I could sense that she was not experiencing me that way as she described the conditions of her reflections and then pronounced her decision. I could sense this (even though I could not yet speak or think symbolically of what I sensed) by the shift in the timing of her gaze, from the extra micro-second hold of a hyperactive scan (a brief pause to which I typically would find myself responding with either a verbal observation or private reflection about her indecisiveness and her seeming to rely on me for some kind of confirmation or direction), to the longer and slower shifting formation of a "sly" smile, marking a shift in rhythm and meaning. This rhythmic marker, forming into a facial display, a very particular kind of smile, created in me a sense of joy and liberation. The beliefs and practices that had haunted Frannie's sense of herself *as wrong* had been loosened, and Frannie seemed to know that she was engaging me in this liberation process. She seemed confident that I would not do or say the *wrong* thing. And the shift in the rhythm of our facial dialogue helped me to feel a similar shift from a concern for my being *wrong* in the judgments coming from my psychoanalytic culture, to a feeling of vitalizing release and openness to the unknown of the liberating consequences of her sense of agency. Here in this micro-moment, the exchange of our smiles catalyzed a shift for both Frannie and me concerning the systems of cultural meanings, sanctions and prohibitions that contextualized our interaction.

What if I had not responded to Frannie's sly smile as I did? What if I had persevered in my concern for being *wrong* within the terms of my own psychoanalytic cultural beliefs and practices, for the possibility that I would retraumatize her either with too much empathy or with an enactment of punitive judgment? What if my desire, as well as my culturally shaped belief that Frannie's breaking off in mid-treatment constituted a *wrong* judgment, overpowered and inhibited my response? I have thought a great deal about this possibility. I think that a key factor in how I was experienced by Frannie and how we subsequently understood and worked with this moment was not just what I would say next, but something that emerged unbidden and unformulated (D. B. Stern, 1997) in our embodied dialogue. I believe that if I had not responded spontaneously to the rhythm that formed into Frannie's sly smile with a syncopated rhythm forming into a smile of my own, things might have gone very differently, at least in that moment, on that day. But having responded as I did to the shift in micro-body rhythm to which Frannie's rhythms invited a new pattern, we now constituted a new context in which she was able to shift to a growing sense of her capacity to act as an agent of her passions and retexture the conflicting cultural beliefs and practices she was navigating. And furthermore, my micro-recognition and response in rhythm coordinated with her shift constituted for me a rapid shift from doubt about my response to a sense of surrender (Ghent, 1999) to what we were constituting, now confirmed in her response to my response.

I want to emphasize here that this clinical episode is offered in order to illustrate a critical meaning that non-symbolized embodied communication can have for therapeutic understanding and action. We have now entered a period in which psychoanalytic attention is being directed toward a web of cultural influences including race, ethnicity, gender, sexual preference, age, physical and cognitive (dis) abilities, socio-economic status and regional environmental opportunities/constraints/and dangers. These considerations do not eclipse traditional understandings of conflict and dissociation, but rather relocate the meanings of such experience within complex nonlinearly unfolding macro- and micro-contextual influences. (I develop this perspective further in Chapter 6).

It is interesting to note that passion and custom are often difficult to reconcile. Freud's representation of these forces in one's intra-psychic experience with the concepts of id and superego accurately \depicted this challenge to psychic equilibrium (Freud, 1923). But Freud's emphasis was more on the constricting, annihilating internalizations that cultural expectations catalyze and not so much on the way that culture can offer a kind of holding environment (mother country) of affirmation and security. In Chapter 6, I engage the ways that culture can serve as an annihilating environment for subjective vitality bringing in the rarely attended-to contributions of Frantz Fanon regarding such dynamics. But here, this chapter is offered as part of a contemporary effort to further unpack the range of meanings and implications that cultural belief, practice and custom can have on subjective experience, with particular emphasis on the navigation and expression of affect as it is either sanctioned or exiled by cultural norms.

Scarry (1985) has written about the political use of physical and psychic torture to impose annihilating effects of pain on the body, erasing the capacity to represent and reflect on experience. (Grand has addressed such annihilating effects in a powerful series of clinical descriptions in her text, *The Reproduction of Evil: A Clinical and Cultural Perspective*, 2000.) The clinical phenomenon taken up here is a product of a set of more subtle coercive effects than intentional physical or psychic torture. This distinction is as important to understanding the ways in which the body registers points of collapse or generative expansiveness for clinical attention in psychoanalysis as is an understanding of the distinction made in discussions of the effects of racism, between overt acts of violence and the kinds of unconscious, and often dissociated, subtle forms of institutionalized and customarily reinforced practices that have come to be recognized for their annihilating impact on a sense of being human and valued by others.

The kinds of clinical phenomena taken up in this chapter, then, occur while thinking is still possible, though dissociation and unconscious conflict are central issues in the work with this patient struggling over the effects of events that have constituted a shift in economic status and norms for social conduct. These phenomena are shown to occur in response to the effects of cross-cultural differences impacting experiences of intimacy and commitment in personal and professional realms of the patient's life (which can be as pivotal a kind of socially influenced space for traumatic impact as the strangling effects of a univocal cultural conformity). It seems that as we further unpack the impact of culture on psychoanalytic practice and the emotional suffering of our patients, we need to expand our scope of attention to include the multicultural intersections occurring both within and between persons. These intersectional dimensions of experience add complexity to counter-transferential as well as transferential experience. In Chapter 5, I consider this issue with further development of the micro-moment focus developed and illustrated in previous chapters. In Chapter 6, I consider this issue with a more macro-focus on the potentially unconscious racialized dimensions of psychoanalytic theory as it has evolved. There I consider the effects of these lacunae on meaning and activity both within, and contextualizing, the psychoanalytic encounter.

Chapter 5

The fluidity of emotions and clinical vulnerability

A field of rhythmic tensions

Paradigm change: a revised conception for attunement

Recently, Civitarese and Ferro observed that "already with Bion, and even more with developments that came after him and the transition to an analytic field theory, psychoanalysis underwent a change of paradigm of the kind described by Kuhn (1962)" (Civitarese & Ferro, 2013, p 194). There is still more to be said about the implications of this paradigmatic shift for clinical activity. In this chapter I further unpack the relationship between the dimension of imaginative experience commonly traversed in psychoanalysis with language concerning structure and category and the much less visited, significantly more difficult-to-narrate region of experience concerning the *fluidity* of activation and hedonics (degree of pleasure/pain) that can shape an interactive field. Daniel Stern describes this region of experience with the term *vitality affects* (Stern, 2004). (In Chapter 6 I shift to a more macro focus to return to the unconscious impact of culturally structured beliefs and practices with a particular focus on race.)

Fonagy et al. have used the term *affect* to denote the mentalized representation of emotions and feelings. They distinguish this categorical dimension from a dimension of fluid emotional activity not able to be represented categorically (Fonagy et al., 2002, p 71). They focus their work on "the relationship of early object relations with mentalization through the lens of affects and affect regulation" (2002, p. 65). They offer their detailed, comprehensive analysis of these terms both historically and empirically, in part, to assist psychoanalysis with an understanding of the relationship between the developmental trajectory of a reflective function capacity and pathology. Their work privileges the significance of this reflective function; in contrast, I am here privileging the significance of attention to fluid emotional activity within, and constitutive of, a field of tensions along with formations able to be categorized as objects and object relations. I understand this fluidity as complex and often quite sophisticated in its emotional significance for relational experience, as opposed to an historical and culturally shaped representation of this level of emotional experience as "primitive," a racist assumption I examine critically in the next chapter.

Toward this end, I am proposing that we consider the analytic value of attending to and narrating what D. N. Stern (1971, 2010) called *vitality affects* and what Bucci (1997) has given the term *subsymbolic* dimensions of experience. These concepts signify patterns of experience that occur as a *field of rhythms*. D. N. Stern has referred to this patterning as *temporal feeling shapes* or *temporal contours* (1994, p. 18). Despite the difficulty in recognizing and tracking such levels of exchange, not unlike other types of activity that may not be registered consciously as it is occurring, this interactive patterning is powerful in its impact on the emotional experiences of both interacting participants: originator and recipient. Such patterning is interactively constituted and experienced as micro-second registrations on *embodied* dimensions of communication and attention. These registrations are not able to be categorized with words, for two reasons. First, they often consist of a complexity too dense to parse into structures or symbols as a strategy for narration. Second, they are micro-second registrations, i.e., they often appear and disappear in time spans of less than a second. If they are consciously experienced and/or recognized at all, that experience is fluid and does not lend itself to structure/form/object. The way we are able to recognize and give meaning to this patterning is through a strategy of *process narration* as it is woven together across time and space in contingent relations that form larger pattern/shapes that begin to be recognizable and representable (as discussed in Chapter 3). Such a strategy of process narration becomes a critical product of field theory.

In considering that this level of experience concerns continuous movement, I privilege thinking of energy in motion as a way of understanding within this paradigmatic change. It is different than Benjamin's conceptualization of the rhythmic third (Benjamin, 2004) in that her formulation includes usage of the experience of attunement as similar to empathy and matching of emotional states. In contrast, I revisit D. N. Stern's initial distinction (1985) between empathy and attunement. In his 1985 working of this term D. N. Stern writes,

> Attunement takes the experience of emotional resonance and automatically recasts that experience into another form of expression. Attunement thus need not proceed towards empathic knowledge or response. Attunement is a distinct form of affective transaction in its own right
>
> (Stern, 1985, p. 145)

So for D. N. Stern, emotional resonance is cross-modally enacted complex patterning across different modes of registration, such as directions of gaze, facial displays, gestures, vocal tone or rhythms, etc. This patterning is quite dense and difficult to apprehend.

Stern distinguishes this kind of affective transaction using the term *communion*: "Communion means to share in another's experience with no attempt to change what that person is doing or believing" (1985, p. 148). He then goes on to develop his conception by distinguishing *communing attunements* from *purposeful misattunements* and *nonpurposeful misattunements*, concluding that "the attunement *process* itself occurs largely unawares" (1985, p. 149). Here D. N. Stern's use of the term *communion* seems quite close to Ghent's use of the term *surrender* (Ghent, 1999), with an emphasis on emotional resonance. In surrender there is active participation that functions paradoxically, not to *act on* but rather to *be receptive to* the experience of the other. At the same time, D. N. Stern's placing of an attunement process out of awareness seems inconsistent with his distinctions of *purposeful* and *nonpurposeful*, which imply some degree of intentionality similar to what occurs with empathy.

Here's how I would further develop these ideas. D. N. Stern's parsing of attunement into three categories, *communing, purposeful* and *nonpurposeful* served as a set of operationally defined categories for observing and analyzing infant/caregiver interactions. His development of the relation between attunement and empathy is somewhat confusing as described above. I think that is why I, Benjamin and others have continued to use the terms interchangeably. I imagine that were D. N. Stern able to engage in further conversation with us to develop a sense of the distinctions and relationship between these two important terms, we might possibly renovate the concept of attunement.

The renovation I propose would shift the term *attunement* from denoting a specific point of matching (attunement) or mismatching (misattunement) to implying a continuous process taking place within a field that consists of a range and combinations of matching and mismatching, all registering cross-modally. The issue of match and mismatch is clarified with the process observations offered by Tronick and Cohn (1989) in their reported observations of infants and caregivers. Both are critical for secure attachment. In fact time and space for mismatch seem critical to the transitionality of experience necessary for continued movement and growth in relationship. So attunement constitutes an interactive patterning of matching and mismatching across different modalities (maybe a *polyrhythmic* third as part of Benjamin's perspective).

Thus, attunement can be understood as a condition of the interactive field shaped by the degree of hedonics and intensity that is moving toward or away from form/category/recognition. But this still leaves the challenge of trying to distinguish a fluid interactive field of movement in terms of hedonics and intensity from the subjective experiences of hedonics and intensity at any point in time by patient or analyst. Clearly subjective experience impacts the interactive field, as the field in turn, in its capacity as an intersubjective space/time continuum of shared experience, impacts subjective experiences of hedonics and intensity. There is continuous movement sustaining and destroying *tensions of varying bearability*. The challenge is to unpack further understanding and develop a strategy for managing the emotional significance of these continuing tensions as movement either toward or away from experiences of form or fluidity.

Within this understanding of attunement and the field, *empathy* then becomes the attempt to create a shared category/state in time, which could serve in the *navigation* of emotional rhythms within a range of intensity and hedonics. I use the term *navigation* rather than *regulation* because the latter implies a kind of control, in contrast to the receptivity occurring with surrender. For empathy to be achieved, experiences of sharing and connection cannot occur for either participant as emotionally too much or too little. Rather, empathic experiences fall within an emotional range bearable enough to be inhabited as shared and moving (as opposed to blocked/negated/destroyed).

Attunement is neither only verbal/explicit or nonverbal/implicit. It can occur on either register. It can be imagined as an always-fluid changing wave, interactively constituting a field having emotional significance concerning intensity and hedonics. These intensities and hedonics range from levels of too much through good enough to too little, always with critical significance for what a subject can bear and recognize, or what she cannot bear and is dissociated from. *Attunement* is constituted by motion. (D. N. Stern liked the metaphor of dance. I like the metaphor of musical improvisation, as in jazz. Both carry the sense of rhythm. Dance privileges embodied communication through physical movement. Music emphasizes the emotional impact of shifting tonalities, sonorities, also an embodied communication, i.e., the morphemic dimensions of speaking/singing including accent, pause, texture, etc.)

Degree of attunement then characterizes the potential for connection/communion or dissociation. It is a characterization of energy in motion. The field can be too turbulent for experiences of recognition leading to emotional connection/communion. Empathy cannot occur outside of a good enough range of attuned hedonics and intensity. Too much or too little can catalyze dissociation and disorganization in either analytic partner or both. It is critical to note that associating attunement too closely with empathy can overlook how dissociation occurs as a field phenomenon, contributing to breakdowns in recognition. The clinical illustrations coming at the end of this chapter illustrate this problem in several ways.

Of what significance do the distinctions between category and fluidity, empathy and attunement, have for analytic activity? First, I suggest we reconsider the developmental significance of embodied experience for clinical work to include: (1) the body as it is attended to or re-presented (symbolized, objectified); (2) the body as a *process* of attention (i.e., body receptivity); and (3) most importantly, the body as communicator of emotional states. Critical to this re-visioning is the distinction between emotional experience generated in infancy and emotional experience occurring in psychoanalytic treatment, where the patient engages with an already developed capacity to re-present with symbol and metaphor absent in infancy Therefore, embodied emotional registrations, often described as somatic (Cornell, 2015) or kinesthetic, emerge with significantly different meanings for the patient in treatment than in infancy. They can fall under the radar of attention because of dissociation but also because of cultural beliefs and practices of privileging or interpolation (i.e., what is given visibility or invisibility, value or abjection). When embodied registrations impact awareness, they are being either quickly or slowly translated into categories (objects) structuring imagination. In the psychoanalytic treatment of patients capable of verbal language activity, often powerfully emotional, nonsymbolized activity can become contextualized by, and interact with, symbolic activity, as I illustrated in Chapter 1. These distinctions are often blurred in clinical efforts to make connections between past and present. Further attention to how this might occur, and with what significance, for the reading of the emotional activity of any clinical field of interaction, is central to the focus of this chapter. To further explore the complex relationship between emotions and how we re-present them or not, I offer some considerations for how the process of symbolization itself, so centrally regarded in psychoanalytic work, can serve to shape and modulate emotional experience.

Symbolization as a form of emotional regulation

In our 2005 text, *Forms of Intersubjectivity in Infant Research and Adult Treatment*, Beebe, Rustin, Sorter and I reported the following relevant empirical observations:

Heller and Haynal (1997) illustrate both procedural and emo-tional implicit knowledge in a paper entitled 'The Doctor's Face: A Mirror of His Patient's Suicidal Projects.' Fifty-nine patients who had attempted suicide in the previous three days were given an initial interview by the same psychiatrist. Two videotape cameras recorded the faces of both doctor and patient. One year later, 10 of these 59 patients made another suicide attempt: the 're-attempter' group. Whereas the psychiatrist's own written predictions were random, fine-grained microanalyses of the videotapes of the psychiatrist's face identified 81 percent of the re-attempters. With her patients who would later try another attempt, the psychiatrist frowned more, showed more head and eye orientation, and showed more overall facial activation and increased speech. This greater activation and negative expressiveness of the psychiatrist can be seen as both regulating her own inner state and communicating with her patient, both out of her awareness (Beebe & Lachmann, 1998, 2002).

(Beebe, Knoblauch, Rustin & Sorter, 2005, p. 6)

It is now commonly acknowledged that analysts continuously navigate (my renovation of the term *regulate*) their own states and communicate with their patients in ways that shift the states of patients without becoming aware of the embodied registrations through which such catalytic communications are carried. An increasing number of analysts are beginning to recognize and clinically report how these dimensions of communication impact the clinical interaction. So how do we understand this process? Are there ways to become aware of such impact that can enhance analytic activity? Clearly, there are emotional experiences that we can bear and some that seem unbearable. How do embodied cues (internal and external) affect the imaginative processes that shape the subjective experience of analyst as well as patient?

It can be extremely helpful for a clinician to consider and reflect on one's own capacity to bear up emotionally or not, and why. It can also be helpful for the clinician to track how her emotional strain can shift throughout a treatment process, in fact, often rapidly within a short segment of a clinical session. One implication of the Heller and Haynal study that they do not explicitly address is how emotional experience unfolds/enfolds as a continuous stream and is not a binary split between bearable and unbearable. The psychiatrist in the study was impacted by, but did not always represent, the distress sensed in the other and registered in her own embodied dimensions. A key question here is whether there are ways we can still use these experiences if not in the immediate micro-moment of their emergence?

What is the threshold of emotional bearability that determines pain and invasiveness at any given moment? When does that threshold trigger a re-presentational process, and when does it trigger dissociation in response to unbearable affect, as seems to have occurred many times in the study? And furthermore, when might emotional unbearability trigger not a representational process and not dissociation, but an embodied response unmediated by symbolic reflection that might open up new possibilities for self and/or relational experience? The determination of emotional unbearability seems to be specific to the time and space in which each individual and other is contextualized and to their specific thresholds for pain and invasiveness. Can this variation in bearability be attributed to history, to constitution? How and when might it be possible for a clinician to recognize this threshold in her own experience and make use of it therapeutically? These are important concerns that we are just beginning to include in our vision of clinical interaction. Whereas pioneers of psychoanalytic technique from Freud to Ferenczi to Reich have increased our understanding of the value of attending to meanings carried in the form of the embodied registrations *of patients*, we are only beginning to develop ways to conceptualize how the analyst might attend to and make use of *her own embodied experience* in the service of analytic work (see Sletvold, 2014 for discussion of Freud and Reich as well as his and others' work (Shapiro, 2009, p. 94) for a discussion of contemporary clinicians working with somatic experience.)

Racker and Reiss

So let me begin to take up the above questions with the following set of considerations. Heinrich Racker's classic set of treatises on psychoanalytic technique recapitulates the conceptual journey of Freud's developing psychoanalytic method, pointing out that a start point for Freud's building out of his work with Charcot was to "give up hypnosis and in its place he urged his patients to remember the forgotten or 'repressed' experiences" (Racker, 1968, p. 8). Racker showed how Freud quickly discovered and began to try to understand the patient's "resistance" to this request, initially recognizing that "resistance arose, above all, from the fact that what should be remembered was painful for the patient, embarrassed him, or was contrary to his moral feelings" (1968, p. 9). Within this perspective, the repressed memory being resisted as painful, embarrassing, or morally shameful concerned infantile emotional experiences involving desire or aggression. The patient then was resisting conscious re-membering of such powerful and shameful emotional experiences. In this last sentence I hyphenate the word *re-membering* as I have the word *re-presenting* to emphasize that this is a reproduction of an experience in a different mode than it originally occurred and that the word is built out of the root word *member,* often used to evoke the body or body parts.

Reminding us of Loewald's contribution regarding this dynamic (Loewald, 1965), Reis suggests a "complex relation (between) ... remembering and repeating" (Reis, 2009, p. 1359). Repeating is generally understood psychoanalytically as a manifestation of symptomatology, an action rather than an integrated symbolic re-presentation of affective experience that could be reflected upon and/or changed, as with re-membering. Repeating is here understood as a symptom resulting from the inability to contain emotionally through re-presentation. But Reis points out that Freud and Breuer also saw a nonconscious aspect to repeating as an affect-motoric expression of memory. In describing the motor phenomena of hysterical attacks in *The Preliminary Communication* (1893), Breuer and Freud wrote that these "can be interpreted partly as universal forms of reaction appropriate to the affect accompanying the memory ... partly as a direct expression of these memories" (Breuer and Freud, 183, p. 15). Reis illustrates how memory was conceived of in Freud's *Project for a Scientific Psychology* (Freud, 1895) "not [as] a cognitive function performed by a conscious subject, but a presubjective physiological change experienced outside of the awareness of the conscious subject" (Reis, 2009, p. 1360). He then goes on to suggest that agreement with Freud and Breuer's view of motor response as a form of memory occurs in contemporary conceptualizations of re-membering as "enactive (Bruner et al., 1966), subsymbolic (Bucci, 1997), procedural (Clyman, 1991) and implicit (Lyons-Ruth, 1998) encoding of information" (Reis, 2009, p. 1361). Here we can see the origins of a *re-presentational* process, as embodied action becomes the foundation for the emergence of symbolic re-presentation in all human interaction, hence, my hyphenation of re-membering.[1]

Now, the genius of Freud's method was the recognition that the struggle with resistance, constituted by the tensions between repeating and remembering, shaped how the analysand would experience and relate to the analyst, i.e., transference. Racker emphasizes that the key fulcrum Freud discovered/created for overcoming resistance to the transference and bringing about the experience of re-membering lay in the analyst's words, i.e., interpretation. "The interpretation is the therapeutic instrument par excellence," writes Racker (1968, p. 33); "only the interpretation can make conscious the unconscious" (p. 38). But as we can see through the lens of Reis's reading of Freud, Breuer and contemporary theoreticians, what is being repeated may not just be resistance. Repeating can be a form of communicating memory. The binary of repeating and re-membering breaks down. Repeating is both a way to not remember and a way to re-member.

Racker seems, in part, to be accepting that making the unconscious conscious—through a process of decoding involving the analysand's associations and the analyst's interpretations—is a form of emotional regulation serving as the central fulcrum of analytic technique. I would ask us to recognize each of the following as strategies of emotional regulation in addition to

Racker's formulation: (1) decoding, with Freud's classical emphasis on understanding drive and drive derivatives; (2) the Kleinian emphasis on recognizing projective and introjective processes; and (3) Bion's process of alphabetizing beta levels of experience so that these can be "contained." Psychoanalytic cure, so often given definition in terms of conscious self-knowledge, has actually always been designed as having an impact on emotional navigation (regulation). The strategy for managing invasive, painful, destructive, dangerous, primitive, primordial emotions has been to create psychological distance and time through *re-presentation* that then precipitates a process of containment facilitative of reflection and self-understanding. Racker struggled with the limits of this understanding and the kind of clinical practice this understanding shaped.

Racker critiqued "classical technique" as "usually more passive" (1968, p. 29), involving less activity, less active interpreting on the part of the analyst. He emphasized that in this sense Freud himself was not a "classic analyst" (p. 29) and clarified that

> to listen well and to empathize have their active aspect too. We *tend* to identify, and identification is, partially, an active mental process, besides implying the reproduction of the object's psychological activity. We let the material penetrate into us and at times the chord which was "touched" vibrates immediately; but at other times this reception must be followed by an active process in which we "touch" and detect what has penetrated in us with our unconscious feeling and thinking, so as to be able finally to unite with it.
>
> (Racker, 1968, p. 29)

And how might we do this? Racker suggests several things. First echoing ideas that were developing concurrently and subsequently to his, particularly in Kohut's self-psychology vision as well as in the work of many Interpersonalists in America, Racker describes how our "task consists ideally in a constant and lively interest and continuous empathy with the patient's psychological happenings" (p. 33), "a straightforward *dialogue*" (p. 35).

Reis and others have offered an innovative conception of the clinician's participation that elaborates Racker's ideas about the analyst's activity in a clinical interaction. This conception has been given the term "witnessing" by Orange (1995), Poland (2000), Grand (2000) and Gerson (2009) as a way to offer guidance for a clinician's attention and activity. These authors are pointing to the enactive impact of the clinician as critical to embodied interaction, something like what Ogden termed "interpretive action" (or "interpretation-in-action") (Ogden, 1994, p. 108) or Hoffman's emphasis on a kind of attention and responsiveness that is non-interpretive and to which he gives the term "non-interpretive interactions" (Hoffman, 1998, pp. xiii–xvi, 182–183). Reis concludes,

> what are often regarded as gaps or lacunae in the verbal, declarative memory of history, I believe, can be reconceptualized as experiences held in episodic memory systems that have no translation into language, but which convey the patient's modes of reaction as memory.
>
> (2009, p. 1362)

Reis further emphasizes that, "The unique context of the psychoanalytic encounter is what allows traumatic repetition to take on the quality of an address rather than remain meaningless reproduction" (2009, p. 1360). Here Reis uses the term "address" as an elaboration of, or amendment to, the term "enactment." *Address* is the way the patient communicates emotionally through interacting with the other/analyst, so the term brings specificity to the concept of enactment by focusing on repetition as an attempt by the patient to use *timing* (*rhythm*) to draw the analyst into what is often an emotionally dysregulated/dysregulating interactive pattern. Rather than framing enactive repetition as pathological, Reis extrapolates the meaning of this as an invitation coming from the patient—a source of hope, if you will—that the clinician will recognize what is enacted as an address, as an embodied form of re-membering, to which the analyst might be receptive and responsive. Here I conceptualize the possible impact of dysregulation, not just as a pathological expression but also potentially as a breaking of an imprisoning pattern, fraught with hope for liberation. (See Saketopoulou (2019) for a discussion of the therapeutic value of dysregulation using a Laplanchian perspective.) Emotional dysregulation and embodied enactment are here experienced as signs of vitality, signals for new possibilities of self-with-other experience.

The concept of witnessing then fits well with Racker's idea of how the analyst should let the patient penetrate his experience so as to vibrate with the chord of the patient's experience. This emotional resonance is Racker's way of describing the analyst's emotional response to the patient's enacted experience. In order to examine the link between the conceptualization of the emotional involvement of analyst and patient offered with a consideration of Racker and Reis, I want to revisit a key term in Daniel Stern's conceptualization of a vitality or fluid dimension of emotional activity, the RIG (acronym for: representations of interaction generalized).

D. N. Stern's concept of RIG revisited

D. N. Stern postulated a process for conceptualizing how interactive experience shapes memory. He ascribed the acronym RIG to this process. Within the perspective I am developing here, the notion of a RIG is critical and transformative to how an analyst attends to clinical process. A RIG is not a categorical object; it is a patterning that can be recognized as its repetition over time becomes an increasingly generalized invariant shape for expected interaction. It is comparable to an object relation, but I would argue more subtle and complex in its algorhythmic accounting for uncertainty than what is generally meant by that term. In other words rather than a particular structure, a RIG is a *range* or *continuum* of possibilities fraught with uncertainty. In contrast to my renovation of the term RIG as a continuum of possibilities, D. N. Stern emphasizes that RIGs are internal representations that metaphorically account for the scope and range of particular relational experiences. For Stern, a RIG is a prototype constituted from specific experiences but ultimately different in subtle detail from any of the experiences it serves to *re-*

present for *re-membering*. So a RIG is not a veridical re-presentation of any particular experience. In that sense it is a fantasy fueled both by past experience and anticipatory hope and/or fear. In other words, a RIG is a process of re-membering, a fantasy of fear and/or hope shaped by and shaping past and future interactive possibilities, which in my vision become not just a structured representation, but rather a continuum.

Here is what I believe D. N. Stern and psychoanalysis have failed to fully explicate. *The invariant patterning of a RIG is constituted by a polyrhythmic weave of vitality affects. It is experience as fluidity, not structure.* A polyrhythmic weave emerges as the stringing or linking together through contingencies of micro-dimensional vitalizing aspects of affect rhythms. These micro-rhythms come to form a larger unit of expected patterning. Such a representation of patterning involving both micro-moments of mismatching as well as matching can shape an often nonlinear dance of possible forms of engagement with varying emotional intensity. Because a RIG involves a range of possibilities and wide variance in emotional impact, it is quite different from a categorical expectation such as the expectation of pleasure or pain (though it might serve as a precursor to this kind of category). In this way, vitality dimensions, when woven together to affect timing and intensity, can impact the emotional tone of a micro-moment of clinical interaction. The emotional significance of any reverie is always shaped more or less consciously by this polyrhythmic weave.

Here it is critical to emphasize that these experiences are not "primitive." Yes, they are based in nonverbal embodied (somatic) modes of registration. But receptivity and communication occur within these modalities in various complex and sophisticated patternings of rhythm (and tonality). Rather than a boundary between such distinctions as explicit/implicit, verbal/nonverbal, symbolic/subsymbolic, such lived experience offers more of a sense of movement through *thresholds* of time and space. Experiences of *thresholds* constitute *tensions of uncertainty* and *thick complexity*. Much analytic work consists of developing capacities to *navigate* and/or inhabit such emotional tensions for the new possibilities that can emerge rather than a collapse into old and inadequate categories of thought or strategies for action. Clearly, re-presentation and reflection concerning projective processes can help with this challenge. The approach offered here serves to expand the impact of such strategies with a recognition of the significance of *continuity* through thresholds, in addition to difference marked by boundaries. Surrendering to this experience of continuity contributes to an emotional sense of connection, recognition, or what D. N. Stern has termed *communion* (D. N. Stern, 1985, p 148). This continuity between embodied and re-presented experience is the basis for my rejecting the historical precedent of considering fluid emotional experience as primitive. To speak of such complexity of information processing as primitive is inappropriate and misleading and is too often rooted in unconscious, culturally carried racialized assumptions as explicated in Chapter 6.

As I just noted, D. N. Stern describes how this patterning is constructed out of a weave of contingencies constituted of affective dimensions tracing vitality. While these dimensions are cross-modal involving gaze, gesture, facial display, rhythms and tonalities, they can also include words. Here the emphasis is on words as experienced on dimensions of vitality, more than just a representational, organizing, or containing function. Words can also be experienced as poetic and/or visceral. They can evoke fluidity in emotion as well as categorization. Depending on how they are used, they can organize or disorganize the bearability of emotional experience. In addition to containment, the emotionally vitalizing impact of words can catalyze the absence of containment, triggering fear, rage, terror, violence and/or dissociation, but also ecstasy and/or a sense of liberation. Such recognition emphasizes the capacity for words/interpretations to be destabilizing, with too much or too little emotional impact. When words destabilize in this way, they are not containing. Further, the absence of containment can have a range of meanings for attunement along dimensions of intensity and hedonics. Given this concern for the emotionally constitutive use of words (Freud's recognition of interpretation) but also emotionally destructive capacity of verbalization/categorization, let's consider Civitarese and Ferro's vision of allowing the patient's inner characters to emerge as in a waking dream for recognition and interaction. In so doing, I am recognizing that, ideally, the analyst is a curious and containing witness. But I am also holding onto the question of what happens when the analyst loses her ability to bear emotional strain and/or cognitively organize the interactive experience in which she is embedded.

A field of emotions, a field of rhythms

Civitarese and Ferro have recently offered an elegant summary of their use of the containment metaphor within an interactive vision for psychoanalysis. I will quote from it carefully in order to clarify the power of this vision and its limits. We can then consider some clinical vignettes to expand these contours.

The authors state that:

> from a field vertex, rather than 'giving interpretations' or 'making interventions' *directed* to the patient, the need is to *attune oneself* to the emotions that are not yet thinkable for the patient and to help him to give shape to them. Attention will then be paid more to the development of the container—that is, to facilitating the growth of the capacity to think—than to its contents.
>
> (Civitarese & Ferro, 2013, p. 207)

Civitarese and Ferro emphasize the need for the clinician to recognize about the patient "the degree of truth about himself that proves *tolerable* to him … his *limits of acceptability*" (p. 207). In this way, the theorists communicate a similar concern and sensitivity captured in D. N. Stern's understanding of attunement processes. They seem to focus on the usefulness of attunement for the analyst's strategies of empathy, clarifying that:

> For this reason, the analyst must pay attention to the derivatives of waking dream thought, as a basis for constantly attempting to apprehend the signals addressed to him by the patient about where he is and how he reacts to what he says (or does not say) to him.
>
> (Ibid., p. 207)

Here their emphasis is on the metaphoric creations imaginatively generated (waking dream thought) by both patient and analyst. For me this approach, while including the analyst's subjectivity, falls short of attention to the analyst's embodied experience and impact on the patient, the registers where emotional fluidity constitutes critically catalytic dimensions of the clinical interaction. Below, I examine an example of this way of working with a patient from Civitarese and Ferro as well as one from the relational tradition as exemplified in the work of Bromberg, and initially in a narrative I offer to characterize a moment of significant embodied address and interaction that illustrates an approach to inhabiting/navigating fluidity along with categorical experiences of object relations. But first, I want to develop some significant points to help guide this exercise in comparison.

For Civitarese and Ferro, "the actual factors of growth" are "the analyst's reveries and affective and visual transformations based on the patient's narration, together with any metaphors that stem from these" (2013, p. 206). This is a powerful and useful vision. But an important emotional dimension of reverie concerns how we understand the analyst becoming afraid, disorganized and dissociated. What happens when the analyst cannot empathize with the patient, as Kohut has conceptualized with his idea of a selfobject failure? What happens when the analyst is not able to recognize the limits of emotional tolerability, not only for the patient but for herself? What happens when the analyst in a state of emotional dysregulation or dissociation is not able to apprehend the signals addressed to him, the importance of which these authors attach to containment and Reis attaches to the act of witnessing the patient's address? As I said above, I am not sure that locating "the actual factors of growth" in the reveries of the analyst takes fully into account the significance of the transformational potentials of the not-contained, non-interpretive, embodied yet catalytic emotional rhythms of interaction that create potential "points of urgency" for growth when the analyst's capacity to think is compromised—as happens more often than the visions offered by Reis or Civitarese and Ferro seem to take into account. Considering this question can lead us to a view that the analyst's subjectivity involves much more than just a witnessing and/or containing function. And so we could ask, does the patient experience the analyst solely as an object serving a containing function, as a porous subject with her own emotional fluidity and vulnerabilities to emotional strain, or both? I am here building a perspective that emphasizes the critical task of taking into consideration the analyst's vulnerability and learning more about how to recognize its manifestations, origins and clinical usefulness. I emphasize attention to embodied registrations of emotional strain for both analyst and patient to be catalytic to this possibility.

Navigating embodied vulnerabilities in both analyst and patient

To better understand our sense of the usefulness of including the analyst's as well as the patient's vulnerability within an interactive vision, I am suggesting it is possible to find a way to begin to recognize and pick up cues indicating vulnerability that might serve to shut down movement in the field of interaction. Toward this purpose, additional metaphors as complementary to, and possibly constitutive of, concepts of containment or even holding can be helpful. While metaphors of containment and holding can be organizing, they can also be constricting, smothering, dominating, or even annihilating, though unintended, particularly to the efforts and self-reflection of training candidates who can easily adapt these conceptual metaphors as performance ideals and then use them for harsh self-assessments. How can we better understand how such unintended effects can occur? First, let's return to the idea of how emotions might be engaged, building on a vision of the field as interactive and thus continuously in motion.

Dimen (2011, p. 5) recruits Foucault to explain how discourse (the exchange of categorical re-presentations) directs attention by its power to include or exclude, reveal or hide, as shaped by cultural beliefs and practices. So, as emotional experience is shifting fluidly, it is made more vivid or obfuscated by cultural categories of privilege or interpellation. This thickness of attention is further complicated as trauma enters into all experience, not just as personal but as cross-generationally transmitted. Analysts and patients are always culture carriers: subjects and subjected. For both analysts and patients, trauma haunts, continuously present and crying out for expression and receptivity in the face of dissociation. Within this vision of the complex and fluidly turbulent tensions of either oppression, liberation, or both, the body's registrations—from micro-movement of face, tone and rhythm of voice, and postural shifts, to larger gestures such as pain and pleasure, loss and desire—are always understood as shaped by, but also capable of subverting, the beliefs and practices of the context in which they emerge. It is interesting here to return to the words of Racker from over a half-century ago, coming from Argentina, where culturally shaped trauma frequently emerged from a toxic tilt, both personally and collectively, within the tensions of oppression/liberation brought over from Europe and repeated in South America. Racker suggests that analytic activity depends on *"our growing capacity to understand and recognize* the unconscious process underlying the patient's *every phrase* and *mental movement*, each silence, each change of rhythm and voice, and each of his attitudes" (1968, p. 22). He gave this active attention the term "analytic microscopy." In his growing recognition and elaboration of countertransference experience, Racker emphasized the analyst's body as well as that of the patient, writing "It is important that the analyst should perceive his own facial expressions, that he should understand them as being a countertransference response to the transference" (p. 27). A related use of miming the patient as self-supervision has been brilliantly theorized and clinically illustrated in the paper "We Got Rhythm," by Nebbiosi and Federici-Nebbiosi (2008). Racker's prescient comments are foundational to D. N. Stern's contributions for psychoanalytic practice, which deeply influenced the Nebbiosis.

Relevant to this vision of body in and of culture, Alvarez suggests that we adapt a metaphor of the infant's shifting gaze as equally foundational to experience as the flow of mother's milk (Alvarez, 1992, p. 79). Scopic impact, seeing and being seen (or not), can be as signifying as vocalization, forming patterns that shape emotionally fluid tensions of loss and desire, potentials for vitality or deadness, identity or diffusion. Gazes of infant and mother, patient and analyst, emerge from and shape multicultural influences, cross-generationally carried as ghosts and/or ancestors contributing to the emotional bearability of any point of interaction (see Harris et al., 2016). Within this expanding vision, the clinician's activity moves beyond just decoding, empathy and containing to include all three *and more*. The analyst's body is subjectively experienced by the patient, but even more importantly by the analyst himself, as a continuously imagined and reimagined, yet interactively connected, influencing Other. Within such fluid ambiguity, the most powerful catalytic impact of the embodied analyst may reside in the range and limits of bearability of her own vulnerability in the navigation of the multicultural uncertainty of such emotional fluency (See Chapter 6 for a further unpacking of this vision). Here, body experiences illuminate vulnerability and the need for self-care. Such experience is also the nexus for subversive forms of agency, new expressions of identity that in turn open new, alternative possibilities for relatedness for the analyst as well as the patient. I use the term "subversive" to describe these new forms of agency, as they emerge from the interactive experience of the clinical encounter, against a cultural context in which they previously were not given space for recognition.

So now we can consider the use and value of this widened scope of attention by examining clinical narratives from different traditions of conceptualization. I first consider a brief clinical narrative from my own experience (see Knoblauch, 2000, pp. 77–89) and then revisit two other brief narratives, one offered by Civitarese and Ferro, reflecting a Bionian field perspective, and the other by Bromberg, reflecting a relational field perspective. I am using these illustrations in order to ground the ideas I have been exploring in observable clinical activity. Note the micro-analytic attention á la Racker and D. N. Stern that my narrative requires, compared to the less frequent micro-focus in the other narratives. Less micro-focus of attention occurs when the motion of embodied registrations is tracked with categorical or structural concepts rather than by way of narration of the tensions constituted within micro-rhythmic patterning. With a structural/categorical lens, few to no opportunities are included for analytic attention to the fluidity of emotional movement and to significances for interactive influence emerging in the embodied dimensions of an encounter. But I am here attempting to demonstrate that it is precisely in these micro-dimensions that indications of vulnerability and porous emotional possibilities emerge for creative clinical work, particularly at times of heightened emotional vulnerability for the analyst. Let's look more closely at the following narratives.

Navigating embodied vulnerabilities in both analyst and patients: three narratives

1. Encountering Sally

When my patient Sally, in shifting her body, seemingly for comfort, crosses her leg to reveal a large rip in her jeans exposing her left buttock, I become tumbled into an inner turmoil, the dizzying pleasure of uncontrolled rushing heat mixed with shame at my response. This is an embodied state interactively precipitated, in which an emulsion of smooth tanned skin, warm slightly open lips and deep inviting eyes draws me into a spin of heightened pulse and heartbeat, deepening my breathing, increasing blood flow with flushing cheeks, tightening of muscles, and images of her naked body entwined with another, as she is describing to me, with a mixed sense of triumph and shame over having seduced the partner of a friend on vacation, and yet having recognized in her own embodied response and his, a new potential to have choice, to regulate the mounting tension and desire – a potential catalyzed within an emerging reflective capacity revealing the meaning that while this felt good, it was not what she wanted. She could speak this, and they could decide not to continue.

This is a scene novel in its twist both to reflection and agency, yet echoing so many she has previously described, coming from "hippie culture," where the enigmatics of sexual play are reduced to a dreamy, "trippy" event too often for the voyeuristic pleasure of another. Here in this blast of seduction described and enacted, our gazes meet as Sally witnesses my emotional contours emerging in breath and face, my struggle with the same desire and vulnerability with which she wrestles in her narrative to me. I am not aware at this point but retrospectively I can wonder about my own past embeddedness in such a time of "hippie culture," when sex and power blurred in ecstatic embodied expression against a cultural background experienced as oppressive. How much does the mix of my emotional experience of that time haunt this scene? I am being surveyed for how I regulate/navigate my mounting tension and desire and begin to restore the reflective capacity that Sally needs me to achieve to recognize her newly emerging efforts to resist anesthetization and dissociation, and rather, bear her desire, shame and vulnerability. In this fragile micro-moment, constituting a shared effort to engage the significance of Sally's traumatic memories and self-destructive patterns of domination and victimization, her visual tracking of my struggle to bear my own desire and vulnerability seems to catalyze a point of agency (urgency) as she experiences her ability to impact my experience of struggle with emotional navigation. My struggle expresses my experience as a witness to her struggle, as well as my struggle with shame and confusion about my past experiences. This moment of interaction precipitates a point of recognition for her (and for me) in what is otherwise a fairly uncertain and therefore frequently confusing, often alarming, flow of embodied emotions. This complexity is constituted in part as her address, her invitation and hope that I might grasp in a good enough way her emotional struggle and in part, by my emotional struggle to be receptive to the flow of her desires and fears concerning her potential to destroy or recognize and commune, to be destroyed or recognized and received.

I offer this brief vignette as an illustration of a way to narrate the process of fluid emotional experience by attending to the rhythmic tensions of emotion scaffolding desire, fear and loss in both patient and analyst. Clearly the tensions constituted for each subject are shaped in part by the rhythmic movement between emotionally unbearable experiences of timing and intensity, too fluid in their velocity of movement to be imagined as some form of predictability, certainty and sense of security within the interactive field. Here, possibilities for a RIG are surging around the field but not yet clear. Here the value of D. N. Stern's distinctions are illustrated as they can expand an analyst's awareness and receptivity within an emotional field, particularly to possible meanings of the emergence of one's own vulnerability. While the following vignettes impress clinically in how they illustrate the thinking behind each stretch of work, neither represent the narrative and clinical value of tapping into the kind of fluid emotional process as illustrated above. I offer some considerations for how and why this is so.

2. Encountering Paolo and his analyst

Civitarese and Ferro (2013), have offered the following clinical narrative.

> Paolo begins his analysis as the good boy that he is. In his first session, he tells me about his attempts to fix his Vespa, which has been lying about forgotten for years. After a number of sessions devoted to this subject, I venture to suggest that 'sometimes a *vespa* [Italian for wasp] will sting.' A prolonged silence emerges.
>
> In the next session Paolo, who has hitherto always come along with a laptop, tells me: "My computer has been struck by lightning and it is literally completely burnt out." So I mitigate the pressure of my interpretations, which was intended to demechanize certain aspects of the patient, but when I later return to a more pungent interpretive regime, there appears "the neighbor who collects weapons and who seemed to be aiming a threatening submachine gun." When I return to a more playful style of interpretation, Paolo mentions the neighbor again, saying that his gun —now he has had a clear view of it!—has a red plug on top of it. It is manifestly a toy weapon, so there is no reason to be worried.
>
> As the analysis proceeds, he tells me about his grandmother's farm, which is populated by a whole menagerie of chickens, ducks, hens, sheep, cows and so on—until one day I ask him if he is not fed up with all these herbivores(!). Paolo at first reacts as if he struck a wave of persecution, but in the final session before the

summer vacation, I am surprised to be given a present of little toy wild animals. On returning from vacation, he discovers, carved into the beams of the ceiling of my consulting room, a five-pointed star, the symbol of the Red Brigades—which neither I nor the patients on the couch had ever noticed in 30 or more years.

I now realize that rage and revolution have entered the room. However, when I try to find the carving again, I cannot focus on it: these aspects of Paolo tend to disappear. On another occasion when he shows me the five-pointed star and the mark of the Red Brigades, I take the opportunity of telling him that he has the eyes of a hawk. In this way, I am substituting the hawk for the lost little sparrow he kept in a cage, about which he had told me at length.

These more intensely passionate aspects make their entry into the sessions, albeit in bleached white form, when he receives a letter from his girlfriend, from whom he has heard nothing for a long time; after a prolonged silence on my part, he comments: "I didn't know whether to tear it up or to open it with the letter opener.

It can thus be seen that the metaphor in the strict sense of the term (as a word-related fact) belongs to the order of the narrative derivatives of waking dream thought, but also that the process whereby it comes into being is the same as that of unconscious thought. The transformation from sensoriality into narrative derivatives is "metaphorical" and conversely the metaphors are narrative derivatives.

(Civitarese & Ferro, 2013, p. 202)

Here Civitarese and Ferro offer a brief narrative of the analyst's experience and use of reverie and metaphor with his patient Paolo. In this illustration of developing unsaturated interpretations (which are not attempts at decoding meaning so much as participations in the waking dream with the patient by interacting with his characters and images), the analyst uses terms to describe his activity such as "I venture to suggest," "I mitigate the pressure of my interpretations," and "I return to a more playful style of interpretation" (p. 200). In these instances, the analyst does seem to be describing some aspects of the tone and rhythm of his voice, but only as these modulate the impact of his interpretations. But as Racker, the Nebbiosis and I would suggest, and I might do, the analyst does not invoke his capacity for reflective awareness of other embodied dimensions of his own presence, such as his facial display, gaze, posture, breathing, or movement. Such attention could reveal much about the analyst's emotional experience within the flow of the interaction and how s/he might be contributing to what is being enacted. Such attention is enhanced by a micro-analytic focus on a brief slice of less than a minute as in my narrative. In this particular narrative emotions are chosen for description from a perspective across a range of different sessions across a much larger unit of time. So while the analyst does seem to reflect some awareness of the emotionally fluid registrations that shape his tone and rhythm in the examples above, I would ask us to consider instances when the analyst's vulnerability is such that he begins to disorganize or dissociate, and to consider what might be happening with emotional fluidity at such points as illustrated in my narrative above. Attention to embodied rhythmic fluidity can signal cues to the analyst concerning his/her possible contribution to what is being enacted, such as aggression in this case.

For example, the analyst tells us he becomes aware of and is able to reflect on the emergence of "rage and revolution." I might ask if embodied fluidity in the analyst could facilitate reflection on "rage and revolution" rather than effecting dissociation or a countertransference counter attack of some kind at this point? From the farm animals to the metaphor of the different birds, the analyst seems to want/need his patient to recognize and own his (the patient's) capacity for rage and revolution. But the patient signals early on that the analyst's attempts at containment with interpretations are experienced as attacks/persecution. How might the analyst become aware of his own emotional turbulence, which could be contributing to his own experiences of rage and revolution? How is the analyst dissociating the symbol on his ceiling for some 30 years or more? Could this dissociation have anything to do with how and when he experienced such emotional turbulence in his own changing socio-political contexts? Were the analyst to attend to his own embodied emotional registrations, their possible personal origins, and not be so consciously concerned with his function to contain, might he begin to wonder about the patient's comments on the intensity of his interpretations and their meaning to the patient rather than quickly modulating them? Could the analyst himself be driven by a form(s) of rage to conduct this treatment as part of the revolution in thinking he is attempting to advance? While Jacobs (1986) has used this kind of reverie to understand his patients' suffering, I am here pointing to the opportunity for us, as analysts, to visit our own emotionally fluid vulnerability as a crucial moment in navigating toward the imagery, the characters and stage drama Civitarese and Ferro focus on.

We might then ask, how in this material can we think about an enactment of rage and revolution? I suggest it is not in the content of categorical affects to be contained but rather in the fluid continuous patterning of emotional rhythms between the analytic pair that the enactment emerges with most intersubjective significance. The analyst navigates/struggles to modulate the intensity (rage and revolution?) of his own attempts to interpret the patient's fear of rage and revolution with metaphors about guns and animals. How might the patient's fear that seems unbearable at times, be impacted by the analyst's fear of the analyst's own rage which is being communicated through the embodied modulation of the analyst's own participation? Could the analyst use such attention to develop emotional navigation strategies through attention to this interaction effect? I am suggesting the clinical usefulness of such an expansion of attention.

In contrast to my narrative and the one just reviewed from Civitarese and Ferro, Bromberg has offered a narrative illustrative of his characteristic relational approach. I use this to illustrate how his unique and clinically effective work creates or forecloses on opportunities for engaging his own as well as his patient's embodied registrations and the emotional significances that might be recognized, with particular emphasis on points of vulnerability.

I offer some speculation about clinical opportunities that a wider attention might precipitate.

3. Encountering Bromberg and his patient

Bromberg describes his work

> with a man for whom the ordinarily routine issue of missed sessions and "makeups" was more complex than I had anticipated, and led to an unexpectedly powerful revelation of his fragile link between selfhood and the continuity of past, present and future. Because of the profoundly dissociated structure of his personality, he was unable to process the physical absence of an object and retain its mental representation with a sense of continuity. It was as if both the object (whether a person or a place) and the self that had experienced it had "died," and nothing was left but a void. His solution, as with many such individuals, depended upon his being able to concretize the events that comprised each day's activity and hold them in rote memory hoping that the cognitive linkage would lead to some experience of self-continuity that would "get by" socially. The one exception to his "laissez-faire" attitude towards life was his determination to "make up" missed sessions. Because I required him to pay for sessions he canceled that were not rescheduled, I believed that his fierce insistence that every session be made up no matter when, had to do with issues of power and money, and I particularly felt this as true because most of our discussions about it felt like thinly veiled power struggles.
>
> I can still recall the moment in which it became clear that something much deeper was at stake. We were in the midst of discussing this issue, once again from our usual adversarial frame of reference, when I noticed that, inexplicably, I was feeling increasingly warm and tender towards him, and even had the fantasy of wanting to put my arm around his shoulder. This peculiar change in my own feeling state then led my attention to something in his tone of voice that I hadn't heard until that moment, and I asked him about it. I said that there was something about how his voice

sounded at that moment that made me feel like a part of him was sad or frightened but couldn't say it, and I wondered whether he might be aware of anything like that going on. He then began to talk in a voice I hadn't quite heard before—a voice that conveyed, hesitantly but openly, the sadness and desperation I had heard only as a shadowy presence. He began to confess, shamefully, what he had never before revealed—that his real need was not for me to reschedule sessions that he canceled, but for me to reschedule all sessions, including sessions that I myself wished to cancel, including legal holidays.

Exploring this with him was no easy matter, because as soon as I became directly engaged with the self-state that held the feeling of desperation and longing he fled from the moment, became dramatically more dissociated, and lost all conscious awareness that his wish had any personal relevance other than revealing his propensity to be "impractical." I then told him what I had been feeling toward him that had led me to hear the part of him that until then I had been ignoring. His eyes opened wider, and little by little he began to speak more freely but now as a frightened and confused child. "If I miss a session ..." he said haltingly, "if I'm not at the session ... I won't know what happened during it .... And if you don't make it up ... I'll never know. I'll never have it again."

(Bromberg, 1998, pp. 275–277)

In the first paragraph of his narrative, Bromberg introduces us to the theoretical lens he is developing and illustrating with this clinical illustration from his first book, *Standing in the Spaces* (1998). He describes this patient's struggle with a sense of self-continuity in time. He shares this as a consequence of the patient's "profoundly dissociated structure of his personality." The use of a structural versus process lens to categorize the patient's experience of self-continuity is not necessarily a problem. But it can allow the practitioner/narrator to gloss the micro-analytic emotional rhythms in both self (analyst) and other (patient) that become significant at heightened moments of emotional vulnerability as seems to be described here. Bromberg foreshadows such a moment for us with his description of the patient's "fierce insistence" around power.

In his second paragraph, Bromberg shifts to a particular clinical moment for us to consider. Here Bromberg focuses his attention on his own emotional experience, particularly as it violated what he typically felt in their "usual adversarial frame." Describing feelings of warmth and tenderness and a fantasy of "wanting to put my arm around his shoulder," he tracks how this feeling state shifted his attention to the patient's tone of voice. Here Bromberg offers us a clear example of the kind of micro-focused attention to one's own as well as the patient's embodied address as Cornell, the Nebbiosis, Racker, Reis, Sletvold, Shapiro and I suggest can be clinically catalytic. Then Bromberg describes to the patient how his attention to tone of voice made him feel that the patient ("a part of him") "was sad or frightened but couldn't say it." The patient's voice then shifts to what Bromberg hears as sadness and desperation, and the patient offers a shameful confession.

Bromberg's clinical decision to recognize and verbalize the patient's emotional experience as it emerged within what is relationally considered an enactment (their usual (repeating) adversarial frame) is a typical relational strategy. His work is made even more compelling by his attention to the micro-embodied dimensions of body and voice (his and his patient's) that formed his recognition of an important shifting of the emotional field.

But in the third paragraph we see a disassembling of what seemed to have been constituted just seconds previously. Bromberg uses the continuous dimension of emotionally fluid experience to illustrate his ideas about self-state shifting and dissociation. He narrates to us how when he told the patient of his warm feelings toward him that had precipitated his observation of the patient's emotional experience, the patient began to speak as a "frightened and confused child." Bromberg uses this clinical vignette as an illustration of dissociation as a "disruption of the experience of time."

I want to emphasize the magnitude of Bromberg's contributions to our understanding of clinical process, and particularly dissociative processes and the appearance and disappearance of self-states in treatment. I also want to clearly emphasize that my comments to follow are not intended as a critique of his contributions, nor of his clinical work here (which is quite brilliant). But I do want to use this particular clinical example to demonstrate the value of bringing attention to micro-process, the emotional fluidity of the interactive field and analytic vulnerability. Here we can ask a series of questions that are not answerable in any definitive way but offer important opportunities for us to deepen the kind of attention to categorical structure and process fluidity that Bromberg's work helps me to develop.

In returning to Bromberg's decision to speak his question/ observation about his and the patient's emotional states, I am wondering, with my retrospective privilege of this point of encounter, whether a different experience for both analyst and analysand might not have unfolded were Bromberg to simply note his and his patient's emotional states as part of an unfolding and fast-moving process (referred to in his text as a disruption/ confusion in time) *and not speak.* I wonder if the emotional dimensions of the field that Bromberg was now recognizing and "hadn't heard until that moment" were not always present but obscured by the repeating "power struggle" pattern Bromberg first describes, a form of interactive re-membering/address (á la Reis's conception) with the patient, of early trauma concerning such basic issues of existence as agency, presence and loss. Were this the case, another strategy for recognition might have been through further attention and reflection to the fluidity of one's own and the patient's emotional rhythms as they constituted and resolved tensions of control/power in their interactive patterning. Such a focus of attention constitutes a critical aspect of surrendering to the impact of the emotional field upon the analyst's struggle to reflect and remain present and agentic without necessarily repeating the power struggle pattern earlier described.

I am wondering here what it is like emotionally for Bromberg (or for any of us) to be the one who requires the patient to pay for sessions he canceled and then to be the one who wants to put his arm around his patient. Here is a marked shift in the analyst's self-states (to use the categorical language of structure) not given further reflection, and I wonder about the analyst's own vulnerability in meeting his patient's. My reverie takes me to my own conflicted feelings around setting boundaries and rules for patients (and others in my life including students, colleagues, friends and family members). I often experience a fast-moving wash, waves of feelings ranging from shame to power. Might Bromberg have experienced similar emotional movement within various stretches of treatment unable to be further articulated until the moment described? He chose to express a feeling of tenderness, which then catalyzed a connection for the patient to feelings of vulnerability. But Bromberg's action/verbalization also contributed to a disassembling/dissociating for the patient. Was this a repetition of a power gradient between the patient and another (here Bromberg)? Might this particular form of enactment have led to further connections and the growth of a sense of self-coherence and agency? From such a perspective, this moment could also be considered as a point of urgency for wittnessing the emotional fluidity/uncertainty/complexity catalyzed within the patient's address. We do not hear.

But what would have happened if Bromberg had further worked, in reverie, the emotional rhythms of the moment? Could such attention have catalyzed the emergence of *his own shame and power needs* (based in a social context of personal identity and cultural imperatives concerning privilege and abjection) before deciding to verbalize? Could the analyst's attention to his own shame and vulnerability, to the self-role congruence or incongruence of privilege and power, have led to a different kind of emotional experience for the patient (and for the analyst)? How might such a shift in attention to the analyst's emotional experience affect the analytic field which the two constituted? I ask these questions, which of course cannot be answered in any definitive way, because through a relational lens an enactment of power was the re-membered address that formed the emotional field first narrated for the reader. Though the narrative brilliantly illustrates the clinical and theoretical focus of the text, the enactment first described seems to be repeated, continuing to shape the tone of the field as the experiences of both analyst and patient flowed emotionally through a range of possibilities moving in and out and again into emotional unbearability. Could this unbearability be as strong for the analyst as analysand? And could attention to embodied registrations occurring within the fluidity of such rhythmic tensions of emotion have helped the analyst to bear shame and vulnerability in a different way, which could have catalyzed a different experience for both analyst and patient?

Concluding reflections

It is with the kinds of questions that I raise concerning the narratives from Civitarese and Ferro and from Bromberg that we can grow our vision for how we, as analysts, narrate and navigate the fluid tensions constituting emotional experiences with our patients. Attention to embodied registrations of emotional experience (as suggested by Racker, 1968; Knoblauch, 1997, 2000, 2005, 2008, 2011a, 2011b; and others such as Cornell, 2015, the Nebbiosis', 2008; Sletvold, 2014; Shapiro, 1996) enacted and not yet re-presented, can provide a point of urgency for reflection and navigation that might help an analyst gain contact with her/his own struggles within the emotional bearability of any micro-moment of clinical encounter. D. N. Stern's recognition of the interweaving of fluid dimensions of emotion and categorical affective experience provides an organizing lens for analytic recovery within emotionally unbearable, disorganized, if not dissociated, moments of encounter. Expanding attention to include one's own emotional vulnerability in this way can open up possibilities for repair and connection, or the intentional sustaining of uncertainty, central to the catalytic activity of the psychoanalytic encounter. Currently our analytic culture still over-privileges cognitive imagining as the ideal for emotional self-control. This kind of privileging too often makes the body either invisible or potentially "primitive," needing to be contained rather than received as a source of credible and useful semiotic meanings. This cultural bias can erase, or at least make opaque, the capacity of the analyst to recognize and make use of his own vulnerability for its therapeutic value.

I believe it is important to understand and recognize our need for our theoretical visions, and the discourses we use to communicate, as emotional life preservers for recognizing and navigating the emotional significance of the unique characters (self-states) and categorical images that fill ours, and our patients', narratives. It is also important to address and develop our understanding for how lost, confused, even terrified we can become when disorganizing or dissociating in the midst of an emotionally dysregulating moment in treatment – the kind of moment that occurs so much more frequently than we have reported in the past. We need to hold on to our visions and discursive categories, to humbly recognize their centrality to our psychic equilibrium, to our self-care, while at the same time sensing their limits and our own vulnerability. These limits seem to invoke a sense of loss of connection between ourselves and others, a gap not possible to bridge or link, and at the same time such limits invoke a continuously renewing hope and faith carried by desire for emotional contact/communion. This sets up a poignant emotional rhythm for which the English language has no symbolic re-presentation, no word. Turning toward Brazil, we find in the Portuguese tradition of poetry and song, *saudade*. The best English translation I have been able to make of *saudade* is an emotional experience of longing or nostalgia for whom or that which is still present. Perhaps this is an emotional experience related to *nachtraglichkeit*, an emotionally compelling experience of the presence of the past, a haunting presence shaping degree of emotional bearability. Or perhaps it is different, in that *nachtraglichkeit* is a mode of understanding, while *saudade* assumes that understanding, if temporarily emergent, is inevitably and repeatedly lost and found in the fluid movement of desire, in the inevitable polyrhythms of emotional life. These emotional rhythms can shape a future of hope as well as of despair. They are available to our reflection if we but expand our attention to include them. We can recognize our vulnerability as well as that of our patients. We can surrender to the possibilities for growth, recognition and liberation that dysregulated emotional moments make possible, for breakthroughs made possible by breakdowns or breakups. Our embodied capacities for receptivity and communion when words fall short are always right there for each of us.

Note

1 In recognition of this originary process of movement between embodied experience and its re-presentation, Bion has offered the theoretical concept of O and Bionians generally consider the re-presentation of O as a necessary re-presentational fiction. Lacan has used the distinctions *Real* for the originary space and *Symbolic* for re-presentations which are failed attempts to capture the *Real* with language. According to Lacan "the symbol manifests in itself first of all as the murder of the thing [which it represents]" (Lacan, 1977, p. 104, my words added in parentheses) or at least a diluting of the emotional impact of the lived/embodied experience of what is being re-presented.

Chapter 6

Fanon's vision of embodied racism for psychoanalytic theory and practice

In this chapter, I add to considerations for embodied experience and vulnerability across the unconscious and the social first raised in Chapters 2 and 4. In Chapter 2, I illustrated how concepts and language from cultural traditions other than European and North American Enlightenment discourses, might expand theoretical perspectives and clinical strategies for understanding unconscious experience and intersubjective experience. In Chapter 4, I focused on how culturally structured beliefs and practices interact with and shape unconscious re-presentations and conflicts around ethical and moral challenges facing a patient, moving between various class and cultural communities. In this chapter, grounding theory in a clinical illustration, I address the contributions of Frantz Fanon concerning race as it manifests in the tensions between the social and the unconscious, often as embodied. Fanon's perspectives and clinical work have not become part of the psychoanalytic canon to which most candidates are exposed as part of their training. This chapter offers evidence for the value of what Fanon has contributed for psychoanalytic work in the social contexts of the 21st century.

The struggle

"For sure, we need to speak to the other. But do we need to speak quite so much about the Other? And maybe we should be ultra-careful when speaking for the Other?" (Samuels, in press). I offer this chapter with the trepidation and awareness Samuels calls us to with the quotation above. Why would my attempt to speak about my clinical work (as a white person), with my patient Waverley, (a black person), in terms introduced by Frantz Fanon be of any value other than to assuage my own racist guilt and shame? This project ultimately reflects Straker's warning, that:

> as psychoanalysts and therapists .... What we intend consciously will usually have an unconscious underbelly ... in the very moment that we wish to assert our humanity and rescue the Other, we may paradoxically be at risk of undermining the Other and reinscribing power relations as we unconsciously require the Other to be in a victim state as a counterpoint to our rescuer state.
>
> (Straker, 2018, P. 297, my emphasis)

And so, with this chapter, I consider an encounter consisting of my phantasies as rescuer in interaction with my patient's victimization, located in a space constructed out of the oppressive economic and political arrangements shaped in great part by racist assumptions and practices. But critically and additionally, I emphasize the "fire" of vitalization that was kindled with attention to my patient's emotional truths and my responses, both registering initially, as embodied rather than verbalized. Critical to the value of this experience has been my considerations of how Fanon (as well as the contributions of several others who are currently reading Fanon in order to further elaborate the significance of his vision), can help me/us to harvest the clinical wisdom possible from such an encounter. This project has facilitated: (a) reviewing the writing process with Waverley, (b) the impact our interactions have had on his capacity to locate and vitalize himself, and (c) how our conversations have contributed to this narrative attempt to re-present and reflect on our process.

The impact of place for Fanon, me and Waverley

Fanon is difficult to read, as his thinking weaves an array of perspectives most powerfully shaped by his experiences. He emphasizes three critical periods. He describes the significance of being a black subject growing up in the colonial culture of

Martinique. Upon this, he overlays his experience of education in Paris where he became socialized in European philosophical, political and medical discourses and practices. Finally, and most significant to his messages, he speaks/writes from his experiences of the Algerian revolution and other liberation struggles in Africa. He was able to reflect on his short life (dead of leukemia at the age of 36) from racialized dimensions of *crushing political violence.* This violence shaped his critical and unique clinical understanding of the *vitality of violence* in the face of annihilating oppression, lack and desperation that hunger and torture invoke in a struggle to live as a human. I believe Fanon's perspectives are relevant to formulations for the impact of traumatic experiences experienced by asylum seekers in our current era. But this is a conversation for a different text.

Fanon's contributions have largely been heralded in terms of postcolonial studies, critical theory and Marxism. His significant critique of European psychiatry and, in particular, psychoanalysis, somewhat considered in those professional communities, has not received recognition as central to theory and practice in the clinical psychoanalytic world. In fact, Frantz Fanon is not a figure – previously exiled from the psychoanalytic world like some, such as Adler, Jung, Reich and Ferenczi – whose efforts are now being returned to the epicenter of our conversations. Fanon never existed for psychoanalysis.

Yet, Fanon introduced a concept of *sociotherapie* based in a vision of *sociogeny.* For Fanon, sociogeny was a theoretical perspective which built on, but eclipsed, the culturally myopic vision of Freud's emphasis on sexuality and competitive aggression (I return to this point later in this chapter). Rather, Fanon read Freud's scope of inquiry as always contextualized in a cultural field valorizing and/or abjecting particular discourses and practices. He emphasized and critiqued the significance of racial prejudice expressed as a hierarchy of development based on comparisons of embodied characteristics, particularly skin color and fantasies of innate differences in physiological capacities. Such racially prejudiced assumptions for human development have ultimately been debunked in the anthropological field in which they first emerged (See Brickman, 2018 for an historical analysis). But they continue to seep into psychoanalytic thought and practice.

As correction and expansion to the racist European assumptions and perspectives he encountered, Fanon offered a theoretical view of suffering that emphasized the capacity of socially enforced oppression to shape clinical trauma emerging from powerlessness and lack. His view of treatment always encompassed the struggle for both oppressed and oppressor to revive a sense of control and power – to find the vitality, if possible, that had been suffocated within the assumptions and practices of oppressive violence. Often and ironically, Fanon understood the rescue of this vitality, similarly to Winnicott through forms of ruthless violence. While history has indulged in a characterization of Fanon's participation in collective revolutionary violence, little has been offered concerning his innovative understanding of the kind of violence, understood psychologically, that liberates vitality. Recently, and toward this end, Swartz (2018) has offered a relevant psychoanalytically based recognition of this relation between Fanon's vision and Winnicott's concept of ruthlessness. This is a kind of violence shaped by and demanding the experience of recognition (Benjamin, 1988, 2004, 2009; Winnicott, 1958b) as central to vitality.

While not embedded in a declared revolutionary struggle, I grew up in the 1950s/1960s context of American racism where oppression and resistance continuously collided in the streets and the press. I have described this context in the introduction to this book. As previously noted, in the northeastern city I inhabited, avenues and streets marked ethnic and racial enclaves, easily recognized but also easily crossed by the youth of which I was one, experiencing the opportunities and, mostly, failures afforded by local and national desegregation policies. This multicultural mix of experiences shaped my confusion and desire to connect with the Other – in this case, my childhood friends whose skin color and socio-economic status differed from mine. On the basketball court, in the classroom, at social dances and other activities, I/we engaged cross-racially. But, always, we returned to our respective ethnically and economically very different neighborhoods. And yet, in Jersey City, our youthful zest for vitality drew us continuously to find increasingly creative ways to cross those "red lines" geographically as well as socially. We were refuseniks, renegades, adolescents oppositionally defiant (as the DSM would erroneously have us categorized) who opposed and resisted the segregation that social, political and economic structures into which we were being socialized would impose. As a sociologically categorized white, my experience of that time continuously haunts my struggle for vitality in tension with cognitive dissociation/emotional deadness as I continue to increase my awareness of this world of subtly and not so subtly reinforced institutionalized white privilege over people of color in which I/we are embedded and often participate in so many ways, frequently without conscious awareness. My struggle to engage with the kind of emotional violence such a power gradient produces for me and others continues. This struggle is here reflected in the clinical encounter narrated with my patient, Waverley, which I am using to help illuminate the value of Fanon's thinking for psychoanalytic practice.

Waverley, like me – though sociologically black – had similar experiences of crossing the invisible yet tangible lines of racial difference in his childhood/adolescence/early adulthood, experienced in a similar but different northeastern community. As the clinical narrative that follows illustrates, Waverley physically crossed racial lines and emotionally suffered confusion similar to mine, but, critically, from the different perspective of an embodied person of color, catalyzing emotional trauma and episodes of depression and rage. My life experience, and particularly clinical work, has brought me to the limits of what a white person can only attempt to understand. In this text I narrate my struggle to find emotional connection with the experiences of a patient of color around this ongoing, and frequently unconscious, set of social normative beliefs and practices as they impact our interactions. My struggle to achieve what Fanon means when he uses the term *human* for such an understanding and emotional connection, shapes both the narration to follow and my effort to write this chapter in the limited terms of a culturally shaped discursive practice with which we, as psychoanalysts, attempt to share our experiences for their clinical value.

A moment of urgent encounter

Waverley enters my consultation space, shoulders slumped, gaze averted. He heads directly for the couch (where he sits). He is seated bending over, holding his head in his hands. He looks up. His facial muscles are tensed and his gaze reflects pain. His gaze is directed (at me). He does not speak. There is a pause. He waits, expecting me to take in his emotional state(s). This is a rhythm we are familiar with. Pauses and accents such as these in our interaction have often shaped moments of tension build-up and release. Waverley often seems to feel more comfortable with this embodied register than with verbal formulations, though he is, at times, quite eloquent, offering clear and cogent reflections. I have learned that when he chooses not to speak with words, he is struggling with the unbearability of his suffering and the rage it catalyzes for him. Waverley has learned that I too am often more comfortable with embodied registers of interaction. (I have learned, over my decades of practice the limits and pitfalls of verbal communication for psychoanalytic work (see Cornell, 2015; Knoblauch, 2017; Levenson, 2003; Saketopoulou, 2019; Sletvold, 2014 for relevant discussions and illustrations of such limits and difficulties)).

I feel an embodied rush as part of this emerging sequence. At times, Waverley will enter with a smile, but not this session. This unexpected difference triggers a shift to hypervigilance for me. I wonder what has happened/is happening. His piercing gaze emphasizes the strength of his distress. In recent sessions he has addressed the strains of his current relationship with Evelyn as it has become increasingly intimate. He has also described the power arrangements of his work setting in which he is currently recognized and valued for his expertise, but also exploited economically. Such examples of exploitation occur particularly when his company faces crises with clients in which Waverley is called on for his expertise as the one who might best resolve the problem at hand. But his time and energy is never fairly recognized and compensated.

In which area of his life is his suffering resonating in this moment with me? The clash of his needs for paternalistic recognition at work, in intimate activity, in our space, historically and now currently with his father who is dying of old age and related medical conditions, flashes into my reverie. My body is tense. My gaze takes him in as his is initially averted, and then rises to meet mine. This meeting of gazes is a signal that it is my turn. It is both a plea for holding and a competitive challenge. From shared readings of an earlier draft of this text, and so, with both Waverley's and my reconstructions of what might be happening here, I reflect the following.

His gaze speaks and I translate the meaning, "So? What? What are you going to be able to say and do? Everyone needs me to hold it together. Well, I am suffering and I'm not sure if I'm going to blow … and blow it!!" (The sense of impending explosion either as an inner or outer violence was vivid in both of our recollections and confirmed in subsequent experiences for him at work as later reflected upon in our interactions.)

For me, this precious "it" that may be lost registers as opaque, complex. I say nothing. My pause is dissolved by Waverley's calm but nevertheless disturbing vocalization which comes now, after this micro-moment of tension build-up. He describes the pressure he feels to find a new apartment. The pressure comes both from the ending of his lease which he does not want to renew since an increase is being requested, and from his and Evelyn's decision to share a living space. His pain seems to present in the form of his expectations for collision with Evelyn's, which constitute an emotionally powerful, difficult-to-bear point in their developing relationship. While Waverley is anticipating the strain of their different uses of space – he being less organized and practical, she being fastidiously tidy and brilliant in her planning and use of space and its contents – … this is not the issue! His eyebrows raise. His head tilts upward as if to announce/signal for me to prepare for a blow. He and Evelyn have been visiting possible rentals in different neighborhoods. They have found a space that's desirable in layout and price. Evelyn loves it. She loves the neighborhood. He likes the neighborhood. It feels comfortable socio-economically. But it does not feel culturally comfortable … for him. As he walks the streets after visiting the space, he notes the rare appearance of a black person like him. Rather, the faces encountered on the street are mostly Latinx, White and Asian. Evelyn is pleased with this set of conditions. The community resonates as a good fit with her multicultural background. He does not want to express his discomfort to disappoint her. They need the apartment. He does not want to disrupt her pleasure with this choice. His forehead is deeply creased with the crunch of the tension that these conflicting conditions constitute.

I inquire about their current location, which he describes as much more clearly a "black" neighborhood, though gentrification has begun to be a critical concern for him as part of a neighborhood group that has formed to discuss and respond to the problems that this change is bringing. If they should move, the vitalizing recognition, coming from the sense of community this organization provides, will be lost and he can anticipate "sticking out" as he comes and goes. I ask him to share more about the pros and cons of each neighborhood (I wonder, employing what I soon learn to be a myopic psychoanalytic theoretical perspective for this moment of encounter, if is he in a paranoid/schizoid place, or can he think from a more depressive position reflecting nuances of advantage and disadvantage?) …. There is a pause …. He looks at me with a piercing gaze, in part disbelief, in part concern, in part annoyance, catalyzing a short circuit to the possibility of direction for reflection I suggest.

> You don't know what it is like to be black and have to walk the streets of a neighborhood not identified with blackness … how others look at you, how their gait and body tension speak a recognition of your presence with looks of suspicion and fear.

I pause. Internally, I erupt into confusion and shame. I should know this ….. I do know about this ……. But, do I?,,,,, Really, can I ever ….. really???? ……. I have been working with Waverley for several years now. We have had open and frank explorations of his experience attending a predominantly white private high school which his professional middle-class parents proudly financed, ... of his experiences dating white women, ... of their often disturbing ways of relating to him as a black male, ... the reactions/responses from others offering gazes shot through with negative judgment, disgust, or even verbalized aggression to the mixed race couples he and his partners constituted – these coming mostly from whites, but also blacks. (Here, I use these racialized terms recognizing them as artifacts of a socially constructed imaginary landscape haunting both of our subjectivities, a normative unconscious (Layton, 2006) constructing categories drawing lines of power, privilege and abjection.) But in this moment, my privilege of not ever having to suffer the experience of being targeted as a body so marked by color, my limits to empathic connection, ... this privileged blindness, ... resonates a deep experience of distance, loneliness, embarrassment and confusion for me. It is not that I can't understand/make sense in terms of theories of psychoanalytic conflict, colonial alienation, and racial violence. Rather, I am trying to balance on the cliff-like edge of an uncanny gap (socially constructed) that cannot be traversed, forever separating Waverley's and my experiences. Waverley stares through this silence directly into my eyes. He waits for me. He witnesses my uncomfortable struggle with my feelings of distance, loneliness, embarrassment, confusion and now, yes, gathering rage and self-hate at my own vulnerability and limitation. We do not speak. But I do purse my lips and express a short, quick breath of acknowledgment. In that moment, I am hoping that Waverley is experiencing my struggle with my loneliness, embarrassment and emotional storms in resonance with his. He seems to sense the limits of my attempts to offer recognition. His pause and gaze seem to acknowledge a confirmation of his expectation that I will not/cannot recognize his experience. (Waverley has confirmed this reading of his embodied registrations, emphasizing the discomfort and confusion his experience of my experience catalyzed for him.)

Now there is a shift. In a strange way, outside of the theory and practice in which I have been trained, this *lack of recognition* (or mis-recognition) catalyzes an opening. This is confounding. This opening seems to emerge from my failure as a psychoanalyst in the context of this performance of power arrangements shaped by colonial assumptions for health, treatment and acceptable conduct. I am the one who should know. Here I come up against the weak, or maybe better understood as, false, premises/understandings assembled for my performance as provider. On what basis am I empowered to offer provision? Are we assuming that as a psychoanalyst I am expected to wield the knowledge power socially constructed for me? Or, as a psychoanalyst am I not expected to frequently find myself at the place in clinical encounter where training fails as a refuge for mentalization and emotional balance, a point of urgency opening up into opportunity for interactive expansion and personal growth for both clinical interactants? Here, Waverley does not seem so upset. Rather, he now seems calm. Is he feeling resignation or confirmation? We have arrived at this, for me at least, painful gap – a lapse in my socially conferred professional power and privilege. Waverley's gaze, one that I experience as a disappointed understanding of my emotional limit, communicates in this way as a reassurance that he is not damaged or abject, that these moments of painfully attempted, failed recognition of his experience by me, are confirming of his sanity. Somehow this breakdown (in my understanding of his experience) seems to offer a form of hope for him. For me this is a strange experience constituting a denseness of emotions confounding closeness/understanding and distance/difference. However temporarily brief, we seem to have fallen/broken into/ trans-formed (?) a space of difference and vitality, constructed by shared vulnerability, rage and humiliation.

I have since reviewed this description of our interaction with Waverley. He has read and subsequently discussed this manuscript with me. What has been most difficult is achieving some sense of confidence with creating a verbal representation of the denseness of our respective emotional experiences. For now, we both feel settled about what and how it is narrated. But of additional importance is how this session seems to have been catalytic to Waverley's emotionally violent explosion on the job some weeks later. The event shook Waverley and he feared it might lead to losing his job or some kind of retaliation. In fact, this event precipitated a series of conversations between him and his supervisor at work, resulting in improved work distribution and previously unexpressed recognition of the value of his work. As of this writing, the place of racism in this event and subsequent discussion remains unaddressed at his workplace.

I offer this description of clinical encounter with Waverley, aware that it is different than Esprey's clinical narratives of her work with Denesh and Thabi where she judges her impact from the perspective of a theory valorizing containment (Esprey, 2017). It is important to emphasize here that containment is not attempted nor assumed to be therapeutically desirable in my encounter with Waverley. This moment and what it represents is not offered as something to be "worked through" or contained. This moment occurs without conscious recognition initially. Empathy and/or recognition cannot occur in such a moment when the analyst is overpowered emotionally and cognitively frozen or disassembled as I was. (See Chapter 5 for a discussion of the conditions in which empathy or recognition can occur or not.) Rather, this moment is offered to illustrate the impact of an unconscious and unintentional, but nevertheless powerful, if not violent, reversal of a power gradient that might otherwise constrict clinical possibility. In my narration this power gradient is shaped by social positions defined within a social discourse mined with implicit and therefore unconsciously constructed racist phantasies. Neither Waverley nor I put much trust in words, though we use them. Our sense of truth more often emerges, as in this narrative, on embodied registers of gaze, breath, rhythmic accents or pauses where there is more fluidity than containment, nevertheless vitalizing.

The encounter is also different than Swartz's clinical narrative of her work with Alphus (Swartz, 2018). The breakdown of recognition here is not an explosion blowing things into smithereens á la Swartz's reading of Winnicott through Fanon. The social categories Waverley and I encounter and perform do not fall apart, as may have been more possible in South Africa at the time of Swartz's text. These categories hold firmly, strangling possibilities for *counter-recognition* within the socially constructed field in which our interaction is shaped and limited. Swartz explains how *counter-recognition* becomes possible when previous categories of alienation are destroyed, leading "to a reconstitution, or in Winnicott's terms dissolution of a world made precarious by object-relating" (Swartz, 2018, p. 526). With Waverley, there is breakdown in recognition, but there is also painfully registered emotional connection in shared response to the absence of reconstitution. Here we find (we found) ourselves in violent intersubjective process. This process carries and re-inscribes structures of imagination as well as unrepresentable trauma, the haunting phantomatic (D. Butler, 2019a) shaping power through racism, from which we would both wish/dream to be liberated.

And so, if one speaks of violence here, it seems to be a violence of *mis-recognition*. But I think what occurred was that the failure of recognition was mutative because it was a failure of a kind of recognition based on a racist order for cognizing, for organizing experience and one's place in it. Stephen Hartman suggests this as a kind of non-recognition leading to an opening in the phantomatic register (Hartman, personal communication August 15, 2019). I take up how this involves the phantomatic in the further discussion of our encounter below. But here I want to emphasize how what occurred served to violate an expectation for a repetition of a power gradient. This violation then reversed the socially constructed power gradient of the patient/clinician relation and vitalized the patient. So, this moment seemed more about violated norms than violence against norms ... but, maybe, it was both.

In such moments of unbearably painful emotional suffering, words (as culturally constructed) often ring hollow in their failure to represent and communicate recognition of the other's experience. In such moments we are not able to be attentive to, or consciously aware of, how we read or are read by others on the registrations of our embodied communication through rhythms of breath, facial display, direction and form of gaze, vocal tone and rhythm, or postural tensions – micro as well as full-bodied rhythms of movement. I would argue that this bias in attention is shaped by a set of culturally constructed rules/assumptions which are reinforcing of the words and images constituting the normative unconscious (Layton, 2006) in which we are symbolically incarcerated. Simply stated, our classical training valorizes words and thoughts, often disappearing the body (either behind the couch or straightjacketed in a frozen position laid out in vulnerability more like a corpse than an embodied being alive with vitality). This approach was initially rationalized as facilitating neutrality of influence and optimization of contact with unconscious processes. Contemporary psychoanalytic perspectives recognize the limits, if not impossibility, of controlling mutual influence in this way. These perspectives demonstrate the potential for such strategies to have unintended retraumatizing effects (See Knoblauch, 2011a). Additionally, such strategies fail to consider how embodied experience and the social surround shape unconscious imagery and power relations. The possible unconscious dynamics of this kind of violation or breakdown in socially normative power relations is taken up again in the discussion section to follow with considerations from recent contributions by Daniel Butler and Francisco Gonzalez. The discussion is built around critical ways to read Fanon, with a particular focus on how normative rules/ assumptions concerning race emerge from and impact unconscious experience. Such unconscious experience can shape bias in psychoanalytic theory and practice. I offer these considerations to contribute to an understanding of the potentially damaging impact of such bias on experiences of recognition whether counter-, mis- or non- recognition, which at times can explode, and at other times may simply, slowly and painfully, trigger open, vulnerable, and in this way critical, opportunities for therapeutic work. Central to my consideration of these limitations for recognition is the liberating potential of the clinician's surrender to their vulnerability as a form of violent breakthrough for the patient's experience of their own sense of vitality. As Swartz observed, this kind of breakthrough can only occur if previous categories of alienation are destroyed, creating space for how relations can reconstitute as different experience of place, one's place in relation to another and to the social context in which one and the other are embedded.

Discussion

a)   Phantomization and lactification in a sociogenic field

In this section I am using aspects of Fanon's vision to bring into focus otherwise hidden/disguised registrations occurring in the narration of my encounter with Waverley. Reading our encounter through the lens of Fanon's perspective illuminates critical ways the interaction between the unconscious and the social is/was catalytic to our experiences. Here I begin to unpack Fanon's conception of what he called the *sociogenic*. The sociogenic includes how the unconscious is structured with images that have been given categorization and hierarchical meaning within a particular social order. The significance of this relationship for reading my encounter with Waverley is the *racist* structuring of that order.

Daniel Butler (2019a) has contributed an important distinction for understanding the sociogenic process in psychoanalytic work that I find useful here. He distinguishes objects of phantasy from ghosts (see Harris et al., 2016). He explains how historical hauntings (ghosts) function as phantoms or the phantomatic (D. Butler, 2019a, p. 146). Rather than internal objects in the imaginative landscape, phantoms erase presence creating a kind of empty space in the capacity to re-present as memory. Something occurred but was traumatically erased. Gonzalez (2019b, p. 160) in discussing this phenomenon likens it with a medical metaphor to the phantom-limb effect. Something seems to be filling the space, but it is an absence of presence. In this wa,y experiences of place, of placement, of displacement between/across imagination and social interaction are blurred if not amputated. And in this way historical experience essential to the structure of identity and agency is disappeared or disguised. This disguise can and does serve the needs of a hegemonic order with whites in power.

Lewis Gordon (Gordon, 1996) addressed the unconscious dynamics to which Butler and Gonzalez give greater focus. I find Gordon's use of Fanon's ideas about how the black body is re-presented within discourses shaped by racist beliefs and practices helpful in building my understanding of my encounter with

Waverley. Gordon uses Fanon's vision to explain unconscious processes nested in a whitened hierarchy of racist beliefs and practices shaping assumptions about the inferiority of the black body. To develop this perspective Fanon introduced the terms *phobogenic object* and *lactification*. Here I want to focus on the significance of these terms and the processes they represent for the encounter between Waverley and myself.

In Gordon's words, Fanon demonstrates the failure of psychoanalysis to "explain the black" (Gordon, p. 76). He emphasizes Fanon's vision of a sociogenic context consisting of "the subjective and the intersubjective, lived-experience of social-historical reality" (Gordon, p. 76). In my use of Fanon's ideas, I distinguish intersubjective experience as mutual influence registering symbolically as image/imagination in contrast to embodied lived registrations that do not register symbolically, at least in the moment of their emotional impact. For our purposes here it is important to note that embodied registrations are frequently shaped by traumatic socio-historical events emotionally experienced as too unbearable for re-presentation/re-membering as symbol/image in intersubjective space. So intersubjectivity depends on the capacity to re-present symbolically and to share an understanding/recognition of symbolic significance. When the emotional impact of experience is unbearable, symbolization does not occur. Rather, as Butler and Gonzalez point out, experience is dissociated/amputated and/or disguised to reduce emotional unbearability. The challenge for understanding my encounter with Waverley concerns how social discourses based in racist beliefs and practices contribute to such a process of blurring or erasure.

Gordon points to Fanon's description of "blackness" as "phobogenic," and "anxiogenic" (Gordon, 1996, p. 79) to demonstrate how the humanity of the black subject is erased. Thus, the black is internalized, stereotypically as a dangerous object and projected as impulsive, embodying uncontrollable, *primitive*, dys- or unregulated emotional experience shaping fear and desire. "What this means is that the black body does not live on the symbolic level in an anti-black world" … and that "their (blacks') alienation is not neurotic" (Gordon, 1996, p. 80).

If the alienation of the black subject is not neurotic, then how might it be understood? Gordon emphasizes that "the context and content of psychoanalytical emergence [what Butler, 2019a, 2019b; Gonzalez, 2019b are calling place], are conditioned fundamentally by the lived-experience of the white" (Gordon, p. 81, my addition in parentheses). Fanon ascribes this whitening to a haunting phantasy of *lactification* (Fanon (Wilcox translation, 1952b/2008), p. 80), the incontestable privilege of being white: a dream/ideal with which all, white and non-white, are unconsciously haunted within a Manichean arrangement of power established to sustain the conscious fantasies and unconscious phantasies of this difference as essential. Richard Wilcox uses this term in place of the term *hallucinatory whitening* offered in the 1967 translation of the text, *Black Skin, White Masks* by translator Charles Lam Markmann (1952a/1967, p. 100). Ta-Nehisi Coates repeatedly refers to this phantasy/hallucination shared by both whites and non-whites as a *dream* of being white in his text *Between the World and Me* (2015 see pp. 130–132). Waverley and I struggle to unpack the impact of this socializing process on our unconscious and intersubjective processes.

My reading of the elaborations of Fanon's vision by Gordon, D. Butler and Gonzalez takes me to how the Freudian model of psychoanalysis fails to include the impact of the socio-historical on the unconscious. Setting the scope of focus for clinical exploration as consisting of triangular and dyadic dynamics, psychoanalysis leaves out the socially constructed field of relations in which intersubjective experience and familial relations are embedded and therefore given shape and category. The implications of this gap concern both the where and the what, constituting how the frame of treatment is experienced by both patient and practitioner. I am here interrogating the *impact of re-presentations emerging from discursive possibilities shaped and delimited by the particular political implications of a theoretical ordering based on racist distinctions.* With Waverley, my attention to embodied registrations helped me to navigate such stereotyping and scapegoating categories that can incarcerate our sense of place, placement or displacement in relation to each other and in the contexts of treatment and the social order in which treatment is embedded/implicated. I engaged this process with attention to how my experience, and Waverley's experience of me, embedded in such a field of racist discourse, might contribute to his experience of himself.

And so, returning to my encounter with Waverley, we might consider how the scapegoating categorization of the black as a nightmare of *primitive* desire driving a dream of lactification would have us reading Waverley's frequent pauses and/or silences as passive-aggressive rage in oppositional defiance. Waverley and I have discussed this stereotypical response to people of color, which he has often observed and experienced. These discussions occurred both before and after the encounter narrated for this text. Carrying, and acting from, such assumptions requires jettisoning attention to, and abjecting the significance of, complex and sophisticated polyrhythmic, embodied, communication/experience. Critical to this point, clinicians report reading emotional confusion and potential for retraumatization in the silence of a patient. At times, this silence is described as containment and at other times as dissociation. But could such silence have a significant and central meaning to a sense of place or displacement for the patient communicated through patterning of accent and pause? If the patient's silence does not signal dissociation or an attempt at containment, what is the patient experiencing/communicating? Could the patient be struggling consciously with how to express emotional experience for which racist social discourse offers no opportunity? Could this experience be about feeling out of place, not being in the right place (with the right person), having no place, not having the right to a place? Or could the patient's silence be an embodied action creating an emotional place, a space for reflection? Could such a move by Waverley, (or other persons of color so understood/misunderstood in this way), be both for their own need to find expression for what the social order would not give opportunity for expression, and also for me/an Other to experience my struggle for recognition of their struggle, which is otherwise, locked out of discursive possibilities between us? Such phenomena seem more about a struggle to find emotional expression than containment. This is an important distinction. A linear model of development, valorizing the one-dimensional flow of speech accompanied by emotional containment, still dominates an understanding of capacities indicative of developmental competence in psychoanalysis. (This linear way of theorizing is currently eclipsed by nonlinear developmental-systems modeling which understands language as a potential elaboration of embodied emotional registration – not always realized – at times, facilitative of, but at critical points in treatment not adequately substitutive for, such emotional communication.)

How might we struggle with the question of whether we are dealing with the absence of verbal representation of emotions as (1) containment or, (2) dissociation? I have learned to expand my analytic attention to embodied cues available to be read as communication of emotions, often reflecting conflict because of their socially normative meanings and/or lack of civil acceptability (see Knoblauch, 2008, 2011, 2017, for illustrations and discussion). These expressions, sometimes aggressive, sometimes bidding for comfort and understanding, are too often not given verbalization/symbolic re-presentation within an intersubjective space of mutually shared avoidance/fear of misunderstanding, breakdown or emotional eruption. So my critical concern here is not with containment or dissociation. This is also more than an issue of empathy, recognition, transference and/or countertransference. Rather, my regnant concern is place, or focus, of attention: a problem with theory unconsciously shaped by cultural beliefs and practices which can amplify or amputate. And so, nonverbal embodied interaction, often shaped by socio-historical (versus dyadic or triadic) context, is too often overlooked within a scope of attention myopically shaped by classical psychoanalytic visions.

Both Swartz (2018) and I (Knoblauch, 2017) have challenged this myopia of attention and its consequent misreadings of heightened emotional expression, often categorized as "anti-social" when such expression is, actually, socially critical to meanings concerning agency and identity (Winnicott, 1958b). I return to Swartz subsequently in this discussion for further elaboration of this critical understanding. But first I consider contributions from Stephens and Marriott which help to develop the significance of the kind of aggression that Swartz and I would understand as a heightened emotional bid for recognition.

b) Epidermalization and petrification in my encounter with Waverley

In this section I use observations from Stephens, Swartz and Marriott to further unpack the interactional effects of the unconscious and the social. Stephens discusses how the significance of skin color or *epidermalization* emerging in the discourse of a racist social structure shapes sense of place and its hierarchical social value. Marriott focuses on the phantomatic effects of Fanon's concept of *petrification* – the way that the social order amputates the historical significance of trauma from conscious memory and replaces it with frozen images of racialized possibilities/ impossibilities for identity and agency. Swartz describes the violence of shattering unconscious phantasy (what Gonzalez describes as the tearing and fraying of the phantasmic fabric ... necessary for "the forces trapped in the phantomatic (to) start to be released" (Gonzalez, 2019b, p. 163)). These elaborations of Fanon's vision help to add depth and complexity to fathoming my encounter with Waverley.

Stephens' Lacanian reading of another critical moment of encounter, this one offered by Fanon, is most helpful here (Stephens, 2018). This is a moment described by Fanon when he is interpellated in the speech of a white child during a chance public encounter. The famous words, "Look a Negro!" are examined in terms of how the gaze of the child translates into words and behavior emerging from the impact of an emotional destabilization catalyzed by skin color. This destabilization registers as affect carried in the child's speech acts and gaze, as well as the resonance/ dissonance from and by Fanon's self-gaze and silent rage as revealed in his text. I use Stephens' close reading of this social encounter, adding to the visible an understanding for the invisible or unconscious layer of experience that seems to have been at work in my encounter with Waverley.

Stephens uses Lacan's conception to distinguish "between seeing blackness as *other* and (as) other*wise*" (2018, p. 311) She writes:

> In this distinction lies the gap between seeing blackness as the source of an essential difference, and experiencing another's racial location as somehow "*off*," awry – uncannily different enough from the self as to produce a fracture in one's own sense of coherence, *but not yet irrevocably and essentially different.* The former phenomenon represents not the fact of difference but rather the *desire for difference*, and has become an inter-cultural condition of possibility for determining the psyches of modern subjects on multiple sides of the color line. ... By contrast, the latter phenomenon, perceiving the other as other*wise* than the self, emerges in and from the traumatic, inter-personal encounters of racialized subjects with each other, and with an uncanny real.
>
> (2018, p. 311)

Stephens' explanation helps to elaborate Fanon's concept of *lactification*, (Fanon, 1952b/2018, p. 311). I harness this observation and broaden the significance of the term, citing further discussion of this significance below. As stated above, I believe that with the term *lactification*, Fanon is highlighting the incontestable privilege of being white: a dream/ideal with which all, including colonizer/occupier and colonized are unconsciously haunted within an arrangement of power established to sustain the (conscious) fantasy of this difference as essential. And so, this (unconscious) phantasy/dream, in coordination with the phantasy of primitivism, is sustained as uncontested, foundational, essential, serving to preserve and protect the assumptions upon which colonial occupation and socialization are justified and sustained. Fanon offers a psychoanalytic reading of this phantasy in the following quote:

> At the level of the unconscious ... colonialism was not seeking to be perceived by the indigenous population as a sweet, kind-hearted mother who protects her child from a hostile environment, bur rather a mother who constantly prevents her basically

perverse child from committing suicide or given free rein to its malevolent instincts. The colonial mother is protecting the child from itself, from its ego, its physiology, its biology, and its ontological misfortune.

(Fanon, 1961, p. 149)

Fanon characterized the effects of this phantasy on the embodied experience of the black subject in the following observation:

In the white world, the man of color encounters difficulties elaborating his body schema ... the data ... [he uses] are provided not by 'remnants of feelings, and notions of the tactile, vestibular, kinesthetic, or visual nature' ... but by the Other, the white man, who ... (weaves) me out of a thousand details, anecdotes and stories.

(Fanon, 1961, pp. 90–91, my addition in parentheses)

Lactification is thus a mystification continuously "coloring" experiences of identity and agency. For experience not to be *otherwise*, the dream of lactification as an ideal based on color of skin must be shattered. This reading seems consistent with my, and Swartz's, emphasis on the importance of recognizing embodied expressions of extreme emotion as central to, either accompanying, but often more essential and direct than, verbal re-presentation of emotion in constituting a sense of connection and shared understanding. I believe this attention to embodied registrations can contribute to "the dismantling of an internal relation of abjection" (Swartz, 2018, 2019, p. 167). Swartz emphasizes: "To escape from 'drowning in contingency' means throwing off the shackles of being apprehended only in terms set out by a persecutory other; to achieve this, an 'invincible dissolution' is needed (Fanon, 1952a)" (Swartz, 2019, p. 167).

My encounter with Waverley required an "invincible dissolution," a shattering of the myth of lactification haunting each of us. In our clinical encounter, Waverley was able to precipitate this experience for both of us, at least momentarily. *Otherness* could not be confined/defined within an order of cultural prescriptions for how to appear and what to understand. These socially constructed expectations, unstated, infected our emotional responsiveness to the psychoanalytic performance in which we were engaged as well as the experiences to which the analytic process brought us for examination. Waverley had to shatter my trust in the psychoanalytic practice of recognition – both my ability to recognize and his to be recognized in his experiences of suffering and vitality. His presentation (both at work, in private life, and in treatment) in a challenge to *otherwise-ness*, expressing emotional control, violating the stereotypic expectations for emotional outburst from persons of color, nevertheless, also created a bind for him concerning how to express the authenticity of his emotional experience, i.e. rage and indignation. I had to be witness to this embodied struggle. In certain ways I was able to embody such witnessing but, of critical significance, as next discussed, is how I was not able to embody this needed witnessing. And so a second shattering occurred that was as much intersubjective and culturally contextualized between us as it was an intra-psychic event for me. This was a shattering of the power tilt between us, which paradoxically made possible a retrieving and re-contextualizing of what might be *a kind of recognition of a mis-recognition*. This occurred as *his recognition of my suffering the limitations of my power to understand* – my professional hubris, if you will (which provided an emotionally vitalizing, rather than deadening experience for him).

I use further observations from Marriott and Butler to illuminate this shattering of re-cognition and its unfreezing impact on emotional experience – a reworking of what is cognized and its impact for the place of relations. To begin, Marriott develops implications for psychoanalytic practice, introducing the process of *petrification* first elaborated by Fanon. He points out that in *The Wretched of the Earth* Fanon uses the term "to refer to a kind of hardening, or of being turned into stone; since the whole effect of colonialism is to mortify the 'culture' … of black embodied life … the sense of wanting to flee or speak but remaining frozen …" (Marriott, p. 68). Here I read Marriott as connecting the processes of epidermalization and petrification. How does he make this connection? Characterizing petrification as "how motor capacity is literally inhibited in the colony" (p. xv), Marriott emphasizes that "Fanon ... links the violence of colonialism to language, visuality and sexuality," (p. 5) suggesting:

> two kinds of psychic violence: the violence that brings fantasy, or dreaming to a halt ... and the violence that allows fantasy to get going, or be discharged, via the vengeful sadistic fantasy, that maintains, confirms, insures the permanence of the racist status quo ....
>
> (p. 52)

(Here Marriott uses the term fantasy rather than phantasy. I believe his distinction between socially constructed beliefs (fantasies) and unconscious imagery (phantasies) is critical to understanding my encounter with Waverley and Fanon's concerns with the myopia of psychoanalytic practice concerning issues of race.)

I use Marriott's observation to further unpack D. Butler's use of the term "phantomatic." Marriott explains that the effect of this violence is "at the level of the phantasm, ... (where) the *real unreality* of life in the colony could be understood ... a group phantasm ... never fully experienced as illusion ... a kind of imaginary evasion ..." (p. 47). Here, I read Marriott connecting the embodied experience of deadness (dissociation?) to the social experience of a violence carried as an unconscious phantasy (the real unreality of life in the colony) functioning as an uncontested cultural truth (carried in language, gaze and desire), deadening hopes and dreams and unleashing sadism, otherwise unimaginable were its objects simply human. In this way we can understand how processes of *epidermalization* and *petrification* become the foundational assumptions undergirding the fantasy of the truth of *lactification*, repeatedly reinforced with sadistic enactments. Each enactment repeats and reinforces the fantasy that blacks are subhuman and thus need to be feared and overpowered. These social expectations and rituals of interpellation then occur outside of the scope of traditional psychoanalytic vision and practice. Traditionally, such expectations might be understood myopically, in terms of developmental trajectories of behavior and emotional control shaped by dyadic and triadic relational experience, too often amputated from attention to the unconscious racist social beliefs and practices shaping such behavior and emotional experience. But Fanon contextualizes developmental trauma, grounding it in a matrix where the unconscious is shaped by the social and vice versa – a process that becomes a vertiginous reciprocity of bi-directional influence.

Marriott characterizes this matrix or field as constituted by "words ... trapped in the corporeal images that captivate the subject ... the petrification of speech and language, dream and desire ..." (p. 62). Here I use his characterization of Fanon's clinical focus as "not simply to make the subject see what is hidden or repressed, but to ... recognize the imaginary dimensions of its history and language" (p. 62). This is a vision wrought from Fanon's experiences of attempting to understand and practice psychoanalytically within the social field of effects constituted by the racist structuralization of power on the unconscious processes of his clinical subjects. Waverley and I are inevitably constituted within such a racist structure and struggle with both conscious (fantasy) and unconscious (phantasy) processes.

Given Fanon's vision, how might Waverley and I engage a process of recognition? Fanon challenges us to account for more than just the dynamics constituting the vulnerabilities of ourselves and our patients in terms of dyadic and triadic developmental history or a hierarchy of stages for emotional mastery. His vision has implications that go beyond the intersubjective construction of doer/done to (Benjamin, 2004), the binary trap from which intersubjectivity theory would liberate us. Recognition becomes problematized by the discursive terms the social order illuminates/disappears/disguises/distorts for possibility, and how these definitions catalyze racial myopia for both analysts and patients. The scope of Fanon's vision includes a historically repeating process of lactification whereby words are empowered to oppress through a hierarchy of categorization for civility/primitivity. Such words, images and gestures shape sadistic fantasies of racially organized power designed to annihilate self-love and feed an impossible dream of lactification for both the disempowered and the empowered.

Waverley's piercing yet compassionately sad gaze in the micro-moment when I invite cognitive reflection concerning the pros and cons of the neighborhoods where he and Evelyn might choose to live, communicates to me an embodied effort to struggle with a kind of emotional freezing (petrification). Is this petrification a response to my lack of understanding, to an absence of emotional responsiveness from me, to a social context shaped by unconscious as well as conscious racist beliefs and practices in which our work and his daily activities are embedded, or all of the above? I do not immediately experience struggle with petrification in his emotional experience. In fact, I am "petrified," frozen emotionally in a micro-moment before the effect of his gaze begins to be absorbed. How does he experience my frozenness? Does my freezing constitute for him a colonizing gaze accompanying my inquiry? Has my inquiry repeated the possibility for the psychoanalytic project to serve a colonial imperative to "work it through" and "get along" in which I can experience gratification in the role of rescuer? Does this "working through" represent a racist phantasy which Gonzalez has described as "what so easily gets disappeared in relation to racialized experience—especially in the well-intentioned but short-sighted and self-serving work done under the banner of whiteness" (Gonzalez, 2019b, pp 160)? Or can we achieve the mutative goal, to "recognize the imaginary dimensions of" Waverley's "history and language," to bear the pain of trauma and rage, to harvest its significance for each of us?

Waverley's gaze merging rage, sadness and compassion begins to initiate me into an awareness, catalyzing my fear, shame and loneliness. He needs/wants me to recognize *his struggle* and in a certain sense, he recognizes *my struggle* with my limits to recognize him outside of the social discourse that forms the context of our encounter. How can I see/experience him as continuously annihilated because he is black … because of his skin color and the fantasies associated with, and phantasies categorizing, that embodiment without reducing this image by repeating racializing processes of epidermalization and petrification that are carried and reinforced within the emotionally anesthetizing sociological categories of "male" and "black?" How can I see him, as Fanon would offer hope for, as a human suffering within this racist sociogenic context? How can I understand his pain coming from his recognizing my failing him ... as I fail to recognize the complexity of his suffering and my colonizing gaze within the terms and limits of our imaginary capacities, myopically structured by the power arrangements that brought us together? While my writing this may help *me* to some extent with my struggle, how can such a reflective exercise contribute to helping Waverley in his struggle to be experienced beyond stereotype and scapegoat, beyond victimhood to vitality?

In the moment I narrate for you, the reader, there is only struggle, uncertainty and attempts at sensitive navigation of emotional suffering on the part of each of us. Retrospectively, I understand this as a moment of relational tension not to be worked through with "empathy" or "recognition" but rather for *surrender* to vulnerability, a surrender to be born within the social context traumatically impacting our attempt at emotional connection. There are no victories ... some glimmers of vitality for each of us ... but still, continued victimhood for both of us, incarcerated by the language and customs of oppression, the sociogenic field for the registration of our experiences.

Butler asks whether "the clinic can bring national phantoms into existence by the analyst surrendering to some destruction of the clinical setting to which they adhere" (Butler, 2019b, p. 175). In my encounter with Waverley, I found myself surrendering to Waverley's destruction of the power gradient that constructs the clinical "place" phantomatically as safe and recuperative. This previously unacknowledged power gradient disguised the way the clinical space could serve as a place for retraumatization. The shattering of this phantastically driven phantomization for clinical structure/place made space for an embodied experience of a power shift for Waverley and for me. We have continued to revisit and pursue this unbinding in our work subsequent to this encounter. Our considerations have reshaped fee structure and opportunities for communication between sessions among other dimensions of power in the clinical frame. So one can wonder if place as phantom shattered in this moment. Our encounter could not/should not have been contained (by me or by the socially constructed discourse of psychoanalysis). Something needed to break through and did emerge, initially, registering in the embodied rhythms between us.

Butler goes on to ask

> how 'breaking the frame' is a psychopolitical act, and how coincident with such acts, the analyst's Ferenczian 'elasticity' or Fanonian 'tension of opening' might have psychopolitical effects that exceed the clinical setting alone. Such questions are less about the analyst's survival of a destructive tension than the willingness *not to survive* as a vitalization of that tension itself.
>
> (Butler, 2019b, p. 175)

I think Butler's question sharpens the call to political awareness Samuels puts out to clinicians with his notion of the *inner politician.* (Samuels, 2004, p. 829). Waverley and I have continued to explore the implications of our encounter. These efforts seem to have contributed to his increasing vitalization whereby he has successfully challenged unfair work arrangements/practices and opened up conversations of tension liberating relational possibilities between himself and Evelyn as well as him and me that were previously unavailable, invisible.

My surrender to the embodied impact on me of Waverley's embodied registrations; my failure, or rather willingness not to survive in terms of the socially racist options for power that the psychoanalytic place structured, but to surrender to the shattering moment of our encounter, seemed to assist us in our struggle to recognize the imaginary dimensions of the history and language in which we both were phantomatically incarcerated. This observation can serve to reinforce fantasies and phantasies of myself as rescuer. It could also suggest how my violation of my, and Waverley's, expectations for this psychoanalytic stereotype, my surrender to the power of Waverley's embodied emotional communication in this encounter, contributed to a degree of liberation for both myself and Waverley from the psychopolitical stereotypes that can, and have held us apart in racist alienation. I think it important to hold in tension the ways that both observations are true.

Chapter 7

From where have we come and where might we be going?

Edges to thresholds

This book's chapters represent an odyssey of struggle with narrative for that which continuously falls short in its hoped-for delivery of understanding through clarification. I have offered an effort in which re-presentation with words and categories continuously eludes certainty or consistency. Why is this … has this been so … should this be expected for any approach with which we might proceed?

This struggle to communicate, to connect between you the reader and me, (speaker/writer) – two or more subjects seeking a cognitive/affective resonance – repeatedly arrives at paradox. This paradox emerges as the elusive appearance of something firm and able to be held, simultaneous with the experience of something appearing and disappearing in the same flash of time and space. In my first text, *The Musical Edge of Therapeutic Dialogue* (2000, p. 29), I used the metaphor of smoke rings to try to capture this experience; so maybe not so much a flash as a slow wispy cloudiness dissolving time and timing. There, as I suggest here, this illusion of something present becomes boggled by the experience of something disappearing or trans-forming. To describe such experience is like trying to re-present a dream. It glides and slides in and out of awareness as I struggle to formulate, to re-member and reflect. Here the paradox is carried in my effort to create a title, "the musical edge," when in fact edges never completely emerge or coalesce. Rather, if emergence is even accurate, what seems to become apparent is the experience of movement signaled by a sense of *threshold*. Thresholds signal feint, subtle and difficult-to-detect shifts or changes, fluidly blurring one place/state from and into another, without any clear beginning, middle or ending. Hence, as my thinking in the unfolding descriptions contained in these chapters reflects, I expand a lens for clinical attention from what Ogden, 1989) has pointed to as a kind of paranoid/schizoid form of organization – the creation of clear binaries for distinction, based on Klein's position of the same name. This expansion in attention includes what Ogden innovatively introduces as a form of organization that is nonverbal, pre-symbolic, unformulated (D. B. Stern, 1997) and emerging as embodied registrations.

Within this kind of experience, to which Ogden gives the term *autistic continguous* and D. B. Stern gives the term *unformulated*, I struggle with how to engage emotional registrations of *magnitude* or *intensity* as a necessary condition to emergence. This struggle, often conceived/ discussed as a problem of *perception* (see Merleau-Ponty, 2002), is as much about sustaining psychic balance in the wake of *emotional turbulence*, which often shuts down cognitive processes of representation and perception. In fact, I and others encounter a problem of not just dealing with definition and organization. Rather, as Freud introduced with socially revolutionizing consequences, the experience of *hedonics* (the rise and fall, appearance and disappearance, elusive and delirious palpitations of desire, of sex, often translated to, confused with, or amalgamated with destructive power – death instinct), is always an embodied experience of emotional intensity.

State/state shifts continuous movement – navigation

I wonder whether Freud's central strategy for psychoanalytic praxis – to make what is unconscious conscious – might be misguided. How can I think this? I believe that Freud's method often confuses the promoting of identity/agency with reducing emotional suffering. I am not saying that these goals are unrelated. I am suggesting that facilitating identity/ agency does not necessarily reduce emotional suffering. In fact, in my work with adolescents (as well as many adults), I have found just the opposite! Often, the discourses into which we are socialized (within family patterns and the social norms that contextualize family and individual experience) create ideals carrying narcissistic vulnerability that fuel anxiety and affective destabilization.

The centrality of the cognitive process of symbolization is indispensable to predictability and meaning: two experiences that so many of Freud's and our patients struggle to find and hold as central to identity and relational experience in a social field. This unfolding his-her/story of psychoanalytic praxis reveals an evolution of strategies: from Freud's instructions for interpretation of associations; to Klein's ideas about object representation through projective/ introjective processes; to Bionian strategies for containment of otherwise unmanageable, overwhelming and often traumatizing emotions; to Benjamin's model for struggle to escape the bonds of doer/done-to roles (*objectification*) through processes of recognition in tension with a Winnicottian sense of destruction (hence liberating for *subjective experience*). It is not by chance that Benjamin's (1988) effort emphasizes the experience of bondage initially appearing in her book title in terms of love rather than re-cognition (I purposefully hyphenate this word which valorizes a return to cognition from its absence).

Here, I struggle with the bondage of recognition, if not cognition itself. The theoretical contributions Benjamin initiates, and continues to ride, seem to have the potential to shift our attention from the bondage of *captured understanding* to the possibilities unleashed with/ by the emotional turbulence of fear and desire. But these possibilities for liberation and/or transcendence end up being contingent upon the meanings/terms shaped by a social lens. *The possibility for a third experience seems emergent and formulated, always within a social field.* Might we imagine this emergence not so much as a structured position (a third), but rather as a moving process consisting of engagement with thresholds of uncertainty (possibly involving socially constructed fourths, fifths, or more – confounding in their complexity and fluidity)? Thus we begin to attend, not to edges of distinction but, rather, to thresholds as liminal spaces for new, or previously subverted, emotional connection or re-connection. (Here I am preferring the term re-connection to the term re-cognition, shifting the emphasis from re-presentation to embodied communion.) This formulation signifies structures of experience as brief moments or constricted re-presentations of cohesion/coherence inevitably contextualized and colored by the transformative power of fluid rhythmicity. Such structures and/or categories are the building blocks of safety, security, organization. At the same time, structures and categories constrict and incarcerate within discursive practices that empower and disempower. They help us with the experience of self and with the experience of self-state. But then again, maybe these distinctions are not so distinct. Maybe recognition becomes a form(s) of love. Maybe structure paradoxically liberates fluidity and vice versa in a vertiginous spiral of struggle for subjective vitality.

We can revisit Bromberg's (1998) formulation of state and state shifts in light of this possible resonance between love and recognition; a resonance elevating the power of gaze to shape identity, agency, security/safety and experiences of communion. Bromberg and others (see, in particular, Davies & Frawley, 1994) have expanded and reformulated Kohut's idea of the self-experience of *cohesiveness* with a sophisticated challenge to the illusion/ideal of psychic cohesion. This is consistent with Lacan's sense of the mirror as creating an illusion of coherence against an emotional experience of confusing and threatening inner turbulence (Lacan, 1977, p. 2). This model recognizes the significance of *fragmented (shattered?) or discontinuous experience* as necessary to a more clinically useful model of self-experience. To accomplish this renovation in theory, Bromberg introduces the conception of *self-states.* I would posit that self-states emerge theoretically in psychoanalytic discourse as *structures* of experience. But in fact, the key process for the kind of relational psychoanalytic practice Bromberg offers (as discussed in Chapter 5), is the navigation of *self-state shifts* – an experience of movement and contextualization constituted by the tensions between unconscious and social experience. A self-state's significance emerges out of the degree of intensity created by the shift(s) between one state and another. For self-state and self-state shifts to become recognized, a degree of intensity needs to be modulated to avoid dissociation as a response to unbearable emotional turbulence. When modulation is subverted by dissociation catalyzed by emotional unbearability, then empathy, recognition and/or containment are not a possibility. So, rather than with the attempt to become conscious of, to name and/or interpret the experience of a structured state (which can run the risk of collapsing a complexity of emotional fluidity into one affective term such as fear or anxiety, at the same time failing to contain such emotional experience), the significance of Bromberg's approach and its development in the work of D. B. Stern (1997, 2010, 2015, 2018) comes from its capacity to help us traverse the often upending, if not unbearable, vertigo accompanying movement across/between states.

Given this mind-boggling movement, I arrive at a vision beyond the ideals of interpretation, linear projective processes and/or containment, to the nonlinear challenges of *navigating* waves of emotion, the internal and interpersonal turbulences that contribute to uncertainty, anxiety and/or trauma as well as experiences described as certainty, calmness, pleasure or fulfillment. And these emotional waves always emerge into form(ulation) in terms/ categories delineated and circumscribed by the scope and boundaries of the discursive dimensions of the social field in which such experiences are embedded. Struggling with the tensions between discursive limits and the emotional fluidity of lived experience invokes a process to which I have previously noted D. N. Stern has given the term *communion*. My struggle has led me to recognize the central formative significance of the rhythmic dimensions to experiences of communion.

The rhythms of structure and fluidity

The shift of attention from structure to movement naturally brings into focus the significance of rhythm. Rhythm constitutes transition. The formation and dissolution of patterning is always a fluid process. This continuous rhythmic movement makes it quite impossible to locate where unformulated experience occurs/emerges or begins to precipitate into some form. Within polyrhythmic movement, what appears to behave as structure is continuously precipitating and/or dissolving. From this perspective, the subjective experience of rhythm is not structure but rather fluidity constituted by variation patterned with pauses and accents, sometimes syncopated, sometimes not, emerging as repetition, variation, or a mix of both. While rhythmic experiences register as embodied and not symbolic or representational, they carry significant emotional power often trans-lated verbally in efforts toward communion.

I have struggled to engage and illustrate the significance of this fluidity of micro-rhythmic interplay with written trans-lation in the various clinical vignettes offered in the chapters of this text. I have struggled to illustrate significant points of urgency in the intersubjective field that are marked by pauses and accents in the polyrhythmic patterning of the clinical trans-action. But it is critical that attention to the rhythmic patterning of fluid interplay does not settle for the kinds of theoretical structures I warn against for their capacity to inhibit spontaneous, creative responsiveness between patient and clinician. Attention to the conflicts and resolutions emerging from the tensions of fluid uncertainty is expanded with a widening lens to include not just the interpersonal field, but the macro-field in which the interpersonal is embedded. And that field is constituted emotionally as tensions between the unconscious and the social.

Cultural contextualization and intersectional categories

We were called to focus and attend to the tensions between the unconscious and the social by the clinical and theoretical offerings of Frantz Fanon, among a relatively small number of voices supporting this concern over a half-century ago. In his texts, Fanon offers an array of approaches for recognizing the processes of interpellation that the social effects of power have on individual and relational experience. Fanon emphasizes how the discourses, beliefs and practices of occupation function to collectively reduce a sense of identity, vitality and agency to a singular purpose of domination. This hierarchical arrangement of power is based in categorical illusions of racial difference constructed to represent and reinforce the effects of such a linear and reductive arrangement of power on experiences of identity and agency. Processes of epidermalization, petrification and lactification (as described in the previous chapter), function to devitalize colonized/occupied subjects through fear, dissociation and the perversion of desire (for example, such an alienated subject would dream of being/having white(ness)).

Fanon's contributions have been neglected in our field until quite recently. While concerned with the experience of black populations impacted by such processes, these contributions have significance for all patients and practitioners across the spectrum of epidermal difference, inevitably embedded and shaped within the contexts of unconsciously performed social practices and discourses. These practices and discourses too often interpellate and abject populations categorized as "other", thus, constituting attacks on identities and agencies.

Bodies and social rhythms, recognition and communion

And so, with this text, I have extended an emphasis on embodied dialogue beyond the contours of the clinical encounter in the consultation space, as first addressed in *The Musical Edge of Therapeutic Dialogue*. That text initiated an expansion of attention to the micro-rhythmic activity first signaled for its significance by infant/caregiver researchers. The clinical illustrations offered in that text were narrative attempts to trans-late or trans-duce the denseness of continuous embodied polyrhythmic fluidity. These experiences are difficult to parse and describe emotionally without attention to embodied registrations too opaque, too fast changing and slippery to capture with significations of emotional state. So rather than move toward a language of structure and definition – of recognition – I offered a narrative that traces a process of navigating emotional turbulence. This strategy was/is offered for engaging emotional vulnerability, denied/dissociated/avoided with the hubris of a practice leaning so heavily on the need to understand, to interpret, to *form-ulate*.

In this current text I continued to expand the scope of such a narrative process to add to this micro-expansion a macro-expansion that includes the influences of social discourse and practice on emotional stability/turbulence. I focused in on the way that the polyrhythmicity of embodied exchange is shaped by social expectations and reciprocally shapes social performance. Social performance makes experience visible/invisible in tension with a changing wave of emotional possibilities. These possibilities occur or disappear across a continuum from enlivening/vitalizing to destabilizing/deadening. They emerge in subtle and often difficult-to-detect contours, such as direction or deflection of gaze, and rhythmic shifts in voice or gesture. These possibilities mark or blur rhythmic accents and pauses, pregnant with emotional impact. Such possibilities can also emerge in the tonality and or contextual power of spoken or written words as they function not just to represent, but also as embodied expressions of affect. Such expressions of affect can heighten or diminish a sense of communion.

As I end this text, the following questions emerge. How is communion similar to, or different from recognition? Can recognition be understood intersubjectively without attention to the particular social discourse that allows or abjects the identities and agencies that can be detected with recognition? I would answer the first question, renovating Benjamin's title *Bonds of Love* (1988), and suggest that *bonds of love concern the fluid possibility of communion in tension with the categorical possibility of recognition*. My response to the second question, then, is to emphasize that *bonds of discourse* are created by social categories which inevitably structure the conscious, but also the unconscious, activity of imagination (creation of symbols/images). In this way the scope and boundaries of recognition, however intersubjectively constituted, are always constricted by any particular social discourse and the arrangements of power (valorization/interpellation) that shape it.

As stated earlier, communion is understood as the building block of community, an experience of mutually engaged/constituted patterning and rhythm that can construct safety and security through an availability to be receptive to the difference of an other's experience. But attempts at community are too often undermined by expectations and enactments of horrifying danger and violence. We and our patients carry the cross-generationally transmitted trauma of violence resulting from breakdown in communion and community. Such trauma is often carried phantomatically, as embodied, and not phantastically as images registering unconsciously or consciously. The work of Fanon offers psychoanalysis valuable perspectives for understanding and engaging the impact of such trauma in all of us. Fanon's vision can serve as a platform for psychoanalysts to navigate the inevitable turbulences of emotional complexity associated with the tensions between the unconscious and the social. These tensions too often devolve into fear, aggression, dissociation and/or self-hate coming from or directed at an other. Here we face the aporia of ideals clashing. It is in this vortex of collision where recognition can be blurred with fear, scapegoating and stereotyping, and communion is continuously at risk. How do we navigate the tensions between an ideal of recognition and an ideal of communion/community? Within the struggle constituted by tensions of fear and desire, psychoanalysis can reshape its significance for a 21st century in which the fate of community – locally or internationally – is inextricably woven out of, and determined by, our capacities to navigate the social rhythms carried in our embodied expressions. Our performances can either lead into or away from experiences of communion and recognition.

References

Alfano, C. F. (2005), Traversing the caesura: Transcendent attunement in Budhist mediation and psychoanalysis. *Comtemp. Psychoanal.*, 41: 225–247.

Altman, N. (1995), *The analyst in the inner city: Race, class, and culture through a psychoanalytic lens.* Hillsdale, NJ: The Analytic Press.

Altman, N. (in press), *Whiteness: Psychoanalytic explorations.* New York, NY: Routledge.

Alvarez, A. (1992), *Live company.* London: Routledge.

Anderson, F. S. (1998), Psychic elaboration of musculoskeletal back pain: Ellen's story. In: L. Aron & F. S. Anderson (eds.) *Relational perspectives on the body* (pp. 287–322). Hillsdale, NJ: The Analytic Press.

Anderson, F. (2008), *Bodies in treatment: The unspoken dimension.* New York, NY: The Analytic Press, Taylor and Francis Group.

Aron, L. (1996), *A meeting of minds: Mutuality in psychoanalysis.* Hillsdale, NJ: The Analytic Press.

Aron, L. (1998), The clinical boy and the reflexive mind. In: L. Aron & F. S. Anderson (eds.) *Relational perspectives on the body.* (pp. 3–37). Hillsdale, NJ: The Analytic Press.

Aron, L. & Anderson, F. (1998), *Relational perspectives on the body.* Hillsdale, NJ: The Analytic Press.

Atwood, G. E. & Stolorow, R. D. (1993), *Faces in a cloud.* Northvale, NJ: Jason Aronson Inc.

Baranger, M. & Baranger, W. (1961–1962), La situacion analtica como campo dinamico. *Rev. Urag Psicoanal*, 4(1): 3–54.

Baranger, M. & Baranger, R. D. (2008), The analytic situation as a dynamic field. *Int. J. Psycho-Anal.*, 89: 795–826.

Bass, A. (2003), "E" enactments in psychoanalysis: Another medium, another message. *Psychoanal. Dial.*, 13: 657–675.

Bass, A. (2007), When the frame doesn't fit the picture. *Psychoanal. Dial.*, 17: 1–27.

Beebe, B. (2005), Faces-in-relation. Forms of intersubjectivity in an adult treatment of early trauma. In: B. Beebe, S. Knoblauch, J. Rustin & D. Sorter (eds.) *Forms of intersubjectivity in infant research and adult treatment.* (pp. 89–143). New York, NY: Other Press.

Beebe, B., Knoblauch, S., Rustin, J. & Sorter, D. (2005), *Forms on Intersubjectivity in infant research and adult treatment.* New York, NY: Other Press.

Beebe, B. & Lachmann, F. (1998), Co-constructing inner and relational processes: Self and mutual regulation in infant research and adult treatment. *Psychoanal. Psychol.*, 15: 1–37.

Beebe, B. & Lachmann, F. (2002), *Infant research and adult treatment; Co-constructing interactions.* Hillsdale, NJ: Analytic Press.

Beebe, B. & Lachmann, F. (2002), I*nfant research and qdult treatment.* Hillsdale, NJ: The Analytic Press.

Beebe, B. & Stern, D. N. (1977), Engagement-disengagement and early object experiences. In: N. Freedman & S. Grand (eds.) *Communicative structures and psychic structures; A psychoanalytic interpretation of communication.* New York, NY: Plenum Press.

Benjamin, J. (1988), *The bonds of love; Psychoanalysis, feminism and the problem of domination.* New York, NY: Pantheon.

Benjamin, J. (2004), Beyond doer and done to: An intersubjective view of thirdness. *Psychoanl. Q.*, 73: 5–46.

Benjamin, J. (2009), Psychoanalytic controversies: A relational psychoanalytic perspective on the necessity of acknowledging failure in order to restore the facilitating and containing features of the intersubjective relationship (the shared third). *Int. J. Amer. Psychol. Assoc.*, 53: 693–729.

Bion, W. R. (1977), *Seven servants.* New York, NY: Aronson.

Black, M. J. (2003), Enactment: Analytic musings on energy, language, and personal growth. *Psychoanal. Dial.*, 13: 633–655.

Bollas, C. (1987), *The shadow of the object.* New York, NY: Columbia University Press.

Boston Change Process Study Group. (2005), The something more than interpretation revisited. Sloppiness, and co-creativity in the psychoanalytic encounter. *J. Amer. Psychol. Assoc.*, 53: 693–729.

Boston Change Process Study Group. (2008), Forms of relational meaning: Issues in the relations between the implicit and reflective-verbal domains. *Psychoanal. Dial.*, 18: 125–148.

Breuer, J. & Freud, S. (1893). On the psychical mechanism of hysterical pho-nemenon: A preliminary communication Standard Edition 2, 3–17.

Brickman, C. (2018), *Race in psychoanalysis: Aboriginal populations in the mind.* New York, NY: Routledge.

Bromberg, P. (1998), *Standing in the spaces: Essays on clinical process, trauma & dissociation.* Hillsdale, NJ: The Analytic Press.

Bruner, J. S., Oliver, R. R. & Greenfield, P. M. (1966), *Studies in cognitive growth.* New York, NY: Wiley.

Bucci, W. (1997), *Psychoanalysis and cognitive science: A multiple code theory.* New York, NY: The Guilford Press.

Butler, D. (2019a), Racialized violence and the violence of the setting. *Stud. Gender Psychoanalysis*, 20(3): 146–158.

Butler, D. (2019b), Setting (on) fire: Reply to discussion. *Stud. Gender Psychoanalysis*, 20(3): 171–176.

Butler, J. (1990), *Gender trouble: Feminism and the subversion of identity.* New York, NY: Routledge.

Civitarese, G. (2013), *The violence of emotions: Bion and post-Bionian psychoanalysis.* New York, NY: Routledge.

Civitarese, G. & Ferro, A. (2013), The meaning and use of metaphor in analytic fieldtheory. *Psychoanalytic Inq*, 33: 190–209.

Clyman, R. B. (1991), The procedural organization of emotions: A contribution from cognitive science to the psychoanalytic theory of therapeutic action. *J. Amer. Psychoanal. Assn.*, 39S: 349–382.

Coates, T. (2015), *Between the world and me.* New York, NY: Penguin Random House.

Cohn, J. & Tronick, E. (1988), Discrete versus scaling approaches to the description of mother-infant face-to-face interaction: Convergent validity and divergent applications. *Dev. Psychol.*, 24(3): 396–397.

Cooper, S. H. (2003), You say oedipal, I say postoedipal: A consideration of desire and hostility in the analytic relationship. *Psychoanal. Dial.*, 13(1): 41–61.

Cooper, S. H. (2007), Begin the beguine: Relational theory and the pluralistic third. *Psychoanal. Dial.*, 17: 247–271.

Cooper, S. H. (2008), Privacy, reverie, and he analyst's ethical imagination. *Psychoanalytic Q.*, 77: 1045–1073.

Cornell, W. F. (2011), SAMBA, TANGO, PUNK: Commentary on paper by Steven H. Knoblauch. *Psychoanalytic Dialogues*, 21: 428–436.

Cornell, W. F. (2015), *Somatic experience in psychoanalysis and psychotherapy.* New York, NY: Routledge.

Davies, J. M. (1998), Between the disclosure and foreclosure of erotic transference-countertransference: Can psychoanalysis find a place for adult sexuality? *Psychoanal. Dial.*, 8: 747–766.

Davies, J. M. (2003), Falling in love with love: Oedipal and postoedipal manifestations of idealization, mourning and erotic masochism. *Psychoanal. Dial.*, 13: 1–27.

Davies, J. M. (2005), Transformations of desire and despair: Reflections on the termination process from a relational perspective. *Psychoanal. Dial.*, 15: 779–805.

Davies, J. M. & Frawley, M. G. (1994), *Treating the adult survivor of childhood sexual abuse.* New York, NY: Basic Books.

Dimen, M. (1998), Polyglot bodies: Thinking through the relational. In: L. Aron & F. S. Anderson (eds.) *Relational perspectives on the body.* (pp. 65–93). Hillsdale, NJ: The Analytic Press.

Dimen, M. (2003), *Sexuality, intimacy, power.* Hillsdale, NJ: The Analytic Press.

Dimen, M. (2011), *With culture in mind; Psychoanalytic studies.* New York, NY: Routledge.

Downing, G. (2004), Emotion, body and parent-infant interaction. In: J. Nadel & D. Muir (eds.) *Emotional development: Recent research advances.* (pp. 429–449). Oxford, UK: Oxford University Press.

Downing, G. (2008), A different way to help. In: A. Fogel, B. King & S. Shanker (eds.) *Human development in the 21st century: Visionary ideas from systems scientists.* (pp. 200–220). Cambridge, England: Cambridge University Press.

Ehrenberg, D. B. (1992), *The intimate edge.* New York, NY: W.W. Norton & Co.

Esprey, Y. M. (2017), The problem of thinking in black and white: Race in the South African clinical dyad. *Psychoanal. Dial.*, 27: 20–35.

Fanon, F. (1952a), *Black skin, white masks.* trans. by Charles Lam Markmann (1967), New York, NY: Grove Press.

Fanon, F. (1952b), *Black skin, white masks.* trans. by Richard Philcox (2008), New York, NY: Grove Press.

Fanon, F. (1961), *The wretched of the earth.* trans. by Richard Philcox (2008), New York, NY: Grove Press.

Fairbairn, W. R. D. (1958), On the nature and aims of psycho-analytical treatment. *Internat. J. Psycho-Anal.*, 39: 374–385.

Feldman, R., Greenbaum, C., Yormaya, N. & Mayes, L. (1996), Relations between cyclicity and regulation in mother-infant interaction at 3 and 9 months and cognition at 2 years. *J. Appl. Dev. Psychol*, 17: 347–365.

Ferrari, A. B. (1992), *L'eclissi del corpo*. Rome: Borla.

Fivaz-Depeursinge, E. & Corboz-Warnery, A. (1999), *The primary triangle*. New York, NY: Basic Books.

Fogel, A. (1992), Movement and communication in human infancy: The social dynamics of development. *Hum. Movement Sci.*, 11: 387–423.

Fogel, A. (1993), Two principles of communication: Co-regulation and framing. In: J. Nadel & L. Camaioni (eds.) *New perspectives in early communicative development*. London, UK: Routledge.

Fonagy, P., Gergely, G., Jurist, E. L. & Target, M. (2002), *Affect regulation, mentalization and the development of the self*. New York, NY: Other Press.

Freud, S. (1895), The psychotherapy of hysteria. Standard Edition, 2: 253–305.

Freud, S. (1912), Recommendations to physicians practicing psychoanalysis. Standard Edition. Vol. 12: 109–120. London, UK: Hogarth Press.

Freud, S. (1923), The ego and the id. Standard edition. Vol. 19: 3–66. London, UK: Hogarth Press, 1953.

Fromm, E. (1941), *Escape from freedom*. New York, NY: Henry Holt.

Fromm, E. (1947), *Man for himself*. New York, NY: Henry Holt.

Fromm, E. (1955), *The sane society*. New York, NY: Reinhart & Winston.

Fromm, E. (1962), *Beyond the chains of illusion: My encounter with Freud and Marx*. New York, NY: Open Road, Integrated Media.

Gentile, K. (2007), *Creating bodies: Eating disorders as self-destructive survival*. Mahwah, NJ: The Analytic Press.

Gerson, S. (2009), When the third is dead: Memory, mourning, and witnessing in the aftermath of the holocaust. *Int. J. Psycho-Anal.*, 90: 1341–1357.

Ghent, E. (1999), Masochism, submission, surrender: Masochism as a perversion of surrender. In: S. A. Mitchell & L. Aron (eds.) *Relational psychoanalysis: The emergence of a tradition* (pp. 211–242). Hillsdale, NJ: The Analytic Press. (Original work published 1990).

Glover, E. (1955), The therapeutic effect of inexact interpretation: A contribution to the theory of suggestion. In: *The technique of psychoanalysis*. (pp. 353–366). New York, NY: International Universities Press. (Original work published 1931).

Gonzalez, F. (2019a), Interstitial belonging: Centrifugal force, agression, futurity. Paper presented at 17th Annual Conference of The International

Association of Relational Psychoanalysis and Psychotherapy, Tel Aviv, Israel.

Gonzalez, F. (2019b), Necessary disruptions: A discussion of Daniel Butler's "Racialized bodies and the violence of the setting. *Stud. Gender Psychoanalysis*, 20(3): 159–164.

Gordon, L. R. (1996). The black and the body politic: Fanon's existential phenomenological critique of psychoanalysis. In: L. R. Gordon, T. D. Sharpley-Whiting & R. T. White (eds.) *Fanon: A critical reader.* (pp. 74–84). Oxford, UK: Blackwell Publishers.

Grand, S. (2000), *The reproduction of evil.* Hillsdale, NJ: The Analytic Press.

Gunsberg, L. & Tylim, I. (1998), The body-mind: Psychopathology of its ownership. In: L. Aron & F. S. Anderson (eds.) *Relational perspectives on the body.* (pp. 117–135). Hillsdale, NJ: The Analytic Press.

Guralnik, O. (2011), Ede: Race, the law and I. *Stud. Gender Sexuality*, 12(1): 22–26.

Guralnik, O. (2014a), History disclosed in a nightmare: Response to commentaries. *Paychoanal. Dial.*, 24(2): 167–174.

Guralnik, O. (2014b), The dead baby. *Psychoanal. Dial.*, 24(2): 129–145.

Guralnik, O. (2016), Sleeping dogs: Psychoanalysis and the socio-political. *Psychoanal. Dial.*, 26(6): 655–663.

Harris, A. (1998). Psychic envelopes and sonorous baths: Siting the body in relational theory and clinical practice. In: L. Aron & F. S. Anderson (eds.) *Relational perspectives on the body.* (pp. 39–64). Hillsdale, NJ: The Analytic Press.

Harris, A. (2005), *Gender as soft assembly.* Hillsdale, NJ: The Analytic Press.

Harris, A., Kalb, M. & Klebanoff, S. (2016), *Ghosts in the 21st century consulting room.* New York, NY: Routledge.

Harrison, A. M. (2003), Change in psychoanalysis: Getting from A to B. *J. Am. Psychol. Assoc.*, 51(1): 221–256.

Heller, M. & Haynal, V. (1997), A doctor's face: Mirror of his patient's suicidal projects. In J. Guimon (ed.) *The body in psychotherapy* (pp. 46–51). Basel, Switzerland: Karger.

Hoffman, I. Z. (1983), The patient as interpreter of the analyst's experience. *Contemp. Psychoanalysis*, 19: 389–422.

Hoffman, I. Z. (1998), *Ritual and spontaneity in the psychoanalytic process.* Hillsdale, NJ: The Analytic Press.

Hoffman, I. Z. (2006), The myths of free association and the potentials of the analytic relationship. *Int. J. Psycho-Anal.*, 87: 43–61.

Holmes, D. E. (1992), Race and transference in psychoanalysis and psychotherapy. *J. Psycho-Analy.*, 73: 1–11.

Holmes, D. E. (2016), Come hither, American psychoanalysis: Our complex multicultural America needs what we have to offer. *J. Amer. Psych. Ass.*, 64(3): 569–586.

Ingram, P. (2008), *The signifying body: Toward an ethics of sexual and racial difference.* Albany, NY: State University of New York Press.

Jacobs, T. J. (1986), On countertransference enactments. *J. Amer.Psychoanal. Assn.*, 34: 289–307.

Jacobs, T. J. (1991), *The use of the self.* Madison, CT: International Universities Press.

Jacobs, T. J. (1994), Nonverbal communications: Some reflections on their role in the psychoanalytic process and psychoanalytic education. *J. Amer. Psychoanal. Assoc.*, 42: 741–762.

Jaffe, J., Beebe, B., Feldstein, S., Crown, C. & Jasnow, M., (2001), *Rhythms of dialogue in infancy.* Monographs of the Society for Research in Child Development, Serial No. 265, Vol. 66, No. 2.

Kimble Wrye, H. (1996), Bodily states of mind: Dialectics of psyche and soma in paychoanalysis. *Gender Psychoanalysis*, 1: 283–296.

Kimble Wrye, H. (1998), The embodiment of desire: Relinking the body-mind within the analytic dyad. In: L. Aron & F. S. Anderson (eds.) *Relational perspectives on the body.* (pp. 97–116). Hillsdale, NJ: The Analytic Press.

Knoblauch, S. H. (1997), Beyond the word in psychoanalysis: The unspoken dialogue. *Psychoanalytic Dialogues*, 7: 491–516.

Knoblauch, S. (1999), The third, minding and affecting: Commentary on paper by Lewis Aron". *Psychoanalytic Dialogues*, 9(1): 41–51.

Knoblauch, S. (2000), *The musical edge of therapeutic dialogue.* Hillsdale, NJ: The Analytic Press.

Knoblauch, S. (2005), Body rhythms and the unconscious: Toward an expanding of clinical attention. *Psychoanalytic Dialogues*, 15: 807–827.

Knoblauch, S. (2008), Tipping points between body, culture and subjectivity: The tension between passion and custom. In: F. S. Anderson (ed.) *Bodies In treatment: The unspoken dimension.* (pp. 193–221). New York, NY: The Analytic Press.

Knoblauch, S. (2011a), Conceptualizing attunement within the polyrhythmic weave: The psychoanalytic samba". *Psychoanalytic Dialogues*, 21: 414–427.

Knoblauch, S. (2011b), Body rhythms and the unconscious: Expanding clinical attention within the polyrhythmic weave. In: L. Aron & A. Harris (eds.) *Relational psychoanalysis, volume 5, evolution of process.* (pp. 183–204). New York, NY: Psychology Press.

Knoblauch, S. (2017), The fluidity of emotions and clinical vulnerability: A field of rhythmic tensions. *Psychoanalytic Perspectives*, 14: 283–308.

Kohut, H. (1966), Forms and transformations of narcissism. *J. Am. Psychoanalytic Assoc.*, 14: 243–272.

Kohut, H. (1971), *The analysis of the self.* Madison CT: International Universities Press.

Kuchuck, S. (2014), *Clinical implications of the psychoanalysts's life experience: When the personal becomes professional.* New York, NY: Routledge.

Kuhn, T. S. (1962), *The structure of scientific revolutions.* Chicago: University of Chicago Press.

La Barre, F. (2001), *On moving and being moved: Nonverbal behavior in clinical praytice.* Hillsdale, NJ: The Analytic Press.

La Bare, F. (2005), The kinetic transference and countertransference. *Contemp. Paychoanal.*, 41: 249–279.

Lacan, J. (1977), *Ecrits: A selection.* London, UK: Norton.

Layton, L. (2006), Racial identities, racial enactments, and normative unconscious processes. *Psychoanal. Q.*, 75(1): 237–269.

Leary, K. (1997), Race, self-disclosure, and "forbidden talk": Race and ethnicity in contemporary clinical practice. *Psychoanal. Q.*, 66: 163–189.

Levenson, E. (2003), On seeing what is said: Visual aids to the psychoanalytic process. *Contemp. Psychoanalysis*, 38(2): 277–285.

Lewis, M. & Goldberg, S. (1969), Perceptual-cognitive development in infancy: A generalized expectancy model as a function of mother-infant interaction. *Merrill-Palmer Q.*, 15: 81–100.

Lichtenberg, J. D., Lachmann, F. M. & Fosshage, J. L. (2002), *A spirit of inquiry: Communication in psychoanalysis.* Hillsdale, NJ: The Analytic Press.

Loewald, H. W. (1965), Some considerations on repetition and repetition compulsion. In: J. Lear (ed.) T*he essential Loewald: Collected papers and monographs.* (pp. 87–101). Hagerstown, MD: University Publishing Group.

Lyons-Ruth, K. (1998), Implicit relational knowing: Its role in development and psychoanalytic treatment. *Infant Mental Health J.*, 19: 282–289.

Lyons-Ruth, K. (1999), The two person unconscious: Intersubjective dialogue, inactive relational representation, and the emergence of new forms of relational organization. In: L. Aron & A. Harris (eds.) *Relational psychoanalysis: Volume 2, innovation and expansion*. (pp. 31–349). Hillsdale, NJ: The Analytic Press, 2005.

Markman, H. (2011), Metaphors we live by: Commentary on paper by Steven H. Knoblauch. *Psychoanalytic Dialogues*, 21: 437–445.

Marriott, D. (2018), *Whither Fanon? Studies in the blackness of being*. Stanford, CA: Stanford University Press.

McLauglin, J. T. (2005), *The healer's bent: Solitude and dialogue in the clinical encounter*. Hillsdale, NJ: The Analytic Press.

Merleau-Ponty, M. (2002), *Phenomenology of perception*. trans. by Colin Smith, London, UK: Routledge.

Mitchell, S. (1977), *Influence & autonomy in psychoanalysis*. Hillsdale, NJ: The Analytic Press.

Nancy, J. L. (1986), *The inoperative community*. Minneapolis, Minn: University of Minnesota Press.

Nancy, J. L. (2000), *Being singular plural*. Stanford, CA: Stanford University Press.

Nebbiosi, G. & Federici-Nebbiosi (2008). "We" got rhythm: Miming and polyphony of identity in psychoanalysis. In: F. S. Anderson (ed.) *Bodies in treatment: The unspoken dimension*. (pp. 213–233). New York: The Analytic Press.

Ogden, T. (1989), *The Primitive edge of experience*. Northvale, NJ: Jason Aronson Inc.

Ogden, T. (1994), *Subjects of analysis*. Northvale, NJ: Jason Aronson Inc.

Ogden, T. (1997), Reverie and metaphor. *Int. J. Psychoanalysis*, 78: 719–732.

Orange, D. (1995), *Emotional understanding: Studies in psychoanalytic epistlemology*. New York, NY: Guilford Press.

Orbach, S. (1999), *The impossibility of sex*. London: Allen Lane, Karnac 2004.

Orbach, S. (2003), The John Bowlby Memorial Lecture Part I: There is no such thing as a body. *Brit. J. Psychother.*, 20: 3–26.

Orbach, S. (2004), What can we learn from the therapist's body? Attachment and. *Hum. Dev.*, 6(2): 141–150.

Orbach, S. (2006), How can we have a body: Desire and corporeality. *Stud. Gender Sexuality*, 7(1): 89–110.

Phillips, A. (1997), Making it enough. Commentary on paper by Altman. *Psychoanalytic Dialogues*, 7: 741–752.

Phillips, A. (1999), Promises, promises. *Contemp. Psychoanalysis*, 35: 81–89.

Philipson, I. (2017), The last public psychoanalyst: Why Fromm matters in the 21st century. *Psychoanalytic Perspect.*, 14: 52–74.

Piers, C. (2005), The mind's multiplicity and continuity. *Psychoanal. Dial.*, 15(2): 229–254.

Pizer, S. (1998), *Building bridges: The negotiation of paradox in psychoanalysis*. Hillsdale, NJ: The Analytic Press.

Poland, W. (2000), The analyst's witnessing and otherness. *J. Amer. Psychoanal. Assn.*, 48: 17–34.

Powell, D. R. (2018), African Americans and psychoanalysis: Collective silence in the therapeutic conversation. *J. Amer. Psychoanal. Assn.*, 66(6): 1021–1049.

Quinodoz, D. (2003), *Words that touch: A psychoanalyst learns to speak.* London, UK: Karnac.

Racker, H. (1968), *Transference and countertransference.* Madison, CT: International Universities Press Inc.

Reis, B. (2009), Performative and enactive features of psychoanalytic witnessing: The transference as the scene of address. *Int. J. Psychoanal.*, 90: 1359–1372.

Ringstrom, P. A. (2001), Cultivating the improvisational in psychoanalytic treatment. *Psychoanal. Dial.*, 11(5): 727–754.

Rozmarin, E.(2017), The Social is the unconscious of the unconscious of psychoanalysis. *Contemp. Psychoanalysis*, 53: 459–469.

Rozmarin, E. (2019), Transidentification and the post-collective. Paper presented at 17th Annual Conference of The International Association of Relational Psychoanalysis and Psychotherapy, Tel Aviv, Israel.

Saketopoulou, A. (2019), The draw to overwhelm: Consent, risk, and the retranslation of enigma. *J. Am. Psychoanalytic Assoc.*, 67(1): 133–167.

Samuels, A. (2004), Politics on the couch? Psychotherapy and society— Some possibilities and some limitations. *Psychoanal.Dial*, 14(6): 817–834.

Samuels, A. (in press), Sinking like a stone: Activism, analysis and re role of the academy. In: S. Farah & M. Carter (eds.) *The Spectre of the Other: Jungian and post-Jungian perspectives—Proceedings of the 2017 conference of the International Association for Jungian Studies.* London and New York: Routledge.

Scarry, E. (1985), *The body in pain.* New York: Oxford University Press.

Seligman, S. (1990), What is structured in psychic structure?: Affects, internal representations and the relational self. Chicago, IL: Invited presentation at Spring Meeting, Division of Psychoanalysis (39).

Seligman, S. (2005), Dynamic system theories as a metaframe for psychoanalysis. *Paychoanalytic Dialogues*, 15: 285–319.

Shapiro, S. (1996), The embodied analyst in the Victorian consulting room. *Gender Psychoanal*, 1: 297–322.

Shapiro, S. A. (2009), A rush to action: Embodiment, the analyst's subjectivity, and the interpersonal experience. *Stud. Gender Sexuality*, 10: 93–103.

Sletvold, J. (2012), Training analysts to work with unconscious embodied expressions: Theoretical underpinnings and practical guidelines. *Psychoanal. Dial.*, 22(4): 41–429.

Sletvold, J. (2014), *The Embodied analyst: From Freud and Reich to relationality*. London: Routledge.

Sonntag, M. E. (2006), I have a lower class body. *Psychoanal. Dial.*, 16: 317–332.

Spezzano, C. (1993), *Affect in psychoanalysis: A clinical synthesis*. Hillsdale, NJ: The Analytic Press.

Stein, R. (1991), *Psychoanalytic theories of affect*. London: Karnac Books.

Stephens, M. (2018), Skin, stain and lamella, Fanon, Lacan and inter-racializing the gaze. *Psychoanalysis, Culture Soc.*, 23(2): 310–329.

Stern, D. B. (1997), *Unformulated experience: From dissociation to imagination in psychoanalysis*. Hillsdale, NJ: The Analytic Press.

Stern, D. B. (2010a), *Partners in thought*. New York, NY: Routledge.

Stern, D. B. (2015), *Relational freedom*. New York, NY: Routledge.

Stern, D. B. (2018), *The Influence of the unsaid*. New York, NY: Routledge.

Stern, D. N. (1971), A microanlysis of mother-infant interactions. *J. Amer. Academy Child Psychiatry*, 19: 501–517.

Stern, D. N. (1985), *The interpersonal world of the infant: A view from psychoanalysis and developmental psychology*. New York, NY: Basic Books.

Stern, D. N. (1994), One way to build a clinically relevant baby. *Infant Mental Health J*, 15: 9–25.

Stern, D. N. (2004), *The present moment in psychotherapy and everyday life*. New York, NY: Norton.

Stern, D. N. (2010b), *Forms of vitality: Exploring dynamic experience in psychology, the arts, psychotherapy, and development*. New York, NY: Oxford University Press.

Stern, D. N., Beebe, B., Jaffe, J. & Bennett, S. (1977), The infant's stimulus world during social interaction. In: H. R. Schaffer (ed.) *Studies in Mother-Infant Interaction*. New York, NY: Academic Press.

Stern, D. N. & Gibbon, J. (1979), Temporal expectancies of social behaviors in mother-infant play. In: E. Thomas (ed.) *Origins of the infant's social responsiveness.* Hillsdale, NJ: Erlbaum.

Stolorow, R., Brandchaft, B. & Atwood, G. (1987), *Psychoanalytic treatment: An intersubjective approach.* Hillsdale, NJ: The Analytic Press.

Straker, G. (2004), Race for cover: Castrated whiteness, perverse consequences. *Psychoan. Dial.*, 14(4): 405–422.

Straker, G. (2018), Reaping the whirlwind: Reply to Garth Stevens, Gillian Eagle Margarita Kahn, and Donna Orange. *Psychoanal. Dial.*, 28: 292–301.

Suchet, M. (2007), Unraveling whiteness. *Psychoanal. Dial.*, 17(6): 867–886.

Swartz, S. (2018), Counter-recognition in decolonial struggle. *Psychoanal. Dial.*, 28: 520–527.

Swartz, S. (2019), A mingling of ghosts: A response to Daniel Butler's "racialized bodies and the violence of the setting.". *Stud. Gender Psychoanalysis*, 20(3): 165–170.

Thelen, E. (2005), Dynamic systems theory and the complexity of change. *Psychoanal. Dial*, 15(2): 255–283.

Trevarthen, C. (1993), The self born in intersubjectivity: The psychology of an infant communicating. In: U. Neisser (ed.) *The perceived self: Ecological and interpersonal sources of self-knowledge.* (pp. 121–173). New York, NY: Cambridge University Press.

Tronick, E. & Cohn, J. (1989), Infant-mother face-to-face interaction: Age and gender differences in coordination and the occurrence of miscoordination. *Child Dev.*, 60: 85–92.

Weinberg, M. & Tronick, E. (1994), Beyond the face: An empirical study of infant affective configurations of facial, vocal, gestural and regulatory behaviors. *Child Dev.*, 65: 1495–1507.

White, K. P. (2002), Surviving hating and being hated: Some personal thoughts about racism from a psychoanalytic perspective. *Contemp. Psychoanalysis*, 38(3): 401–422.

Winnicott, D. W. (1958a), Mind and its relation to psyche-soma. In: *Through pediatrics to psychoanalysis: Collected papers.* (pp. 243–254). London, UK: Carnac. (Original work published 1949).

Winnicott, D. W. (1958b), The antisocial tendency. In: *Through pediatrics to psychoanalysis.* (pp. 306–315). New York: Basic Books.

Winnicott, D. W. (1960), Ego distortion in terms of true and false self: In The maturational process and the facilitating environment. (pp. 140–152). Madison, CT: IUP, 1965.

Winnicott, D. W. (1971), Playing: A theoretical statement. In: *Playing and reality.* (pp. 38–52). London, UK: Routledge.

Winnicott, D. W. (1975), Withdrawal and regression. In: *Collected papers, Through pediatrics to psychoanalysis.* (pp. 255–261). New York, NY: Basic Books (Original work published 1954).

Index